AF806539

Management for Professionals

More information about this series at
http://www.springer.com/series/10101

Henk R. Randau • Olga Medinskaya

China Business 2.0

Analyze the Economy, Understand the Society, and Manage Effectively

Springer

Henk R. Randau
Vallendar
Germany

Olga Medinskaya
Giessen
Germany

ISSN 2192-8096 ISSN 2192-810X (electronic)
ISBN 978-3-319-07676-8 ISBN 978-3-319-07677-5 (eBook)
DOI 10.1007/978-3-319-07677-5
Springer Cham Heidelberg New York Dordrecht London

Library of Congress Control Number: 2014954481

© Springer International Publishing Switzerland 2015
This work is subject to copyright. All rights are reserved by the Publisher, whether the whole or part of the material is concerned, specifically the rights of translation, reprinting, reuse of illustrations, recitation, broadcasting, reproduction on microfilms or in any other physical way, and transmission or information storage and retrieval, electronic adaptation, computer software, or by similar or dissimilar methodology now known or hereafter developed. Exempted from this legal reservation are brief excerpts in connection with reviews or scholarly analysis or material supplied specifically for the purpose of being entered and executed on a computer system, for exclusive use by the purchaser of the work. Duplication of this publication or parts thereof is permitted only under the provisions of the Copyright Law of the Publisher's location, in its current version, and permission for use must always be obtained from Springer. Permissions for use may be obtained through RightsLink at the Copyright Clearance Center. Violations are liable to prosecution under the respective Copyright Law.
The use of general descriptive names, registered names, trademarks, service marks, etc. in this publication does not imply, even in the absence of a specific statement, that such names are exempt from the relevant protective laws and regulations and therefore free for general use.
While the advice and information in this book are believed to be true and accurate at the date of publication, neither the authors nor the editors nor the publisher can accept any legal responsibility for any errors or omissions that may be made. The publisher makes no warranty, express or implied, with respect to the material contained herein.

Printed on acid-free paper

Springer is part of Springer Science+Business Media (www.springer.com)

Acknowledgements

Of course, this book would never have been possible without the extraordinary help we received. It is hard to express the thanks and gratitude we have for:

- The truly singular lifestyle and mentality of China that inspired us to research and learn, and has been a source of continuous intrigue
- The tireless efforts of a few fantastic people who really strove to make this project a success: Nicolas Kudeba and Matthew Wolf, who helped us drive this project to completion; Céline Lau, who worked on this project before it even became a book, and whose hard work helped us get a head start; and David Barber, Andreas Beckenbach, Carolin Berlich, Jochen Bialek, Sebastian Hundt, Fu Jingzhong, Hou Hong Juan, Ilene Kennedy-McCarthy, Dennis Liu, Bill Mordecai, Michael Mueller, Johannes Stangenberg-Haverkamp, Frank Raetzer, and Tom Youngblood, who granted their generous assistance during specific stages of the project
- The "insight" experts who have given our book invaluable knowledge and perspective
- Our employer, which assigned us to work in China and made the whole experience possible
- Dr. Ngoctuong Lu and Lawrence Wu, our former bosses, who widened our horizons and opened the door to many secrets
- Our Chinese friends and colleagues who made us feel at home in Suzhou
- Dr. Carol Bacchus-Wermke and Dr. Matthias Wermke—the publication pros who have given us ideas and connections, and were the best sparring partner one could imagine
- Dr. Martin Stark who supported the idea from the beginning
- Family and friends giving us constant support and believing in us
- Last but not least, we thank Springer Publishing, especially Dr. Niels Peter Thomas, who believed in the project from the start, and Dr. Prashanth Mahagaonkar, who gave us great support throughout the process.

Abbreviations

a.k.a.	Also known as
ADBC	Agricultural Development Bank of China
Add.	Additional
AP	Associated party
AQSIQ	General Administration of Quality Supervision, Inspection and Quarantine
ASBE	Accounting Standards for Business Enterprises
B.C.	Before Christ
BoComm	Bank of Communication
BRICS	Brazil, Russia, India, China, and South Africa
BSB	Public Security Bureau
BT	Business tax
CAS	Chinese accounting standards
CCDI	Central Committee for Discipline Inspection
CCP	Chinese communist party
CCTV	China central television
CEIC	Euromoney Institutional Investor Company
CIIC	China International Intellectech Corporation
CJV	Cooperative joint venture
CMC	Central Military Commission
CNY	Chinese Yuan
CPC	Communist Party of China (from 1921)
CPD	Central Propaganda Department
C-SOX	Basic Standard of Internal Control for Enterprises
CT	Consumption tax
CTMO	China Trademark Office
DoJ	Department of Justice
DTA	Double tax agreement
e.g.	Exempli gratia, Latin "for example"
ECID	Economic Crime Investigation Department
EIBC	Export Import Bank of China
EIT	Enterprise income tax
EITL	Enterprise income tax law

(continued)

EJV	Equity joint venture
Etc.	Etcetera, Latin "and so forth"
FAI	Fixed asset investment
FCPA	U.S. Foreign Corrupt Practices Act
FDI	Foreign direct investments
FESCO	Foreign Enterprise Service Corporation
FIE	Foreign invested enterprises
FYP	Five-year plan
GAC	General Administration of Customs
GAPP	General Administration of Press and Publication
GDP	Gross domestic product
GDP PPP	Gross domestic product at purchasing power parity
GLD	Government-linked company
GVA	Gross value added
Hrs	Hours
i.e.	Id est, Latin "which means"
IAS	International accounting standards
IFRS	International financial reporting standards
IIT	Individual income tax
Incl.	Inclusive
IPO	Intellectual property office
IPR	Intellectual property rights
ISP	Internet service provider
JP, DE, U.S.	Japan, Germany (Deutschland), the United States
JSC	Joint Stock Company
JSCB	Joint-Stock Commercial Banks
k, m, bn, tn	Thousand, million, billion, trillion
KMT	Kuomintang (nationalist party)
mil/yr	Millions per year
MoC	China's Ministry of Commerce
MoF	Ministry of Finance
MPS	Ministry of Public Security
MSD	Monthly standard deduction
M&A	Mergers and acquisitions
NBCP	National Bureau of Corruption Prevention
NCA	National Copyright Administration
NOC	Chinese National Oil Company
NPC	National People's Congress
OECD	Organization for Economic Co-Operation and Development
OT	Overtime
PBC	People's Bank of China
PLA	People's Liberation Army
PLC	Publicly listed company
PRC	People's Republic of China

(continued)

R&D	Research and Development
RMB	Renminbi
RO	Representative Office
ROC	Republic of China (Taiwan)
SAFE	State Administration of Foreign Exchange
(S)AIC	(State) Administration for Industry and Commerce
SARFT	State Administration of Radio, Film, and Television
SARs	Special Administrative Regions
SASAC	Assets Supervision and Administration Commission of the State Council
SAT	State Administration of Taxation
SCSC	State Councils Standing Committee
SDBC	State Development Bank of China
SEC	Securities and Exchange Commission
SEI	Strategic Emerging Industries
SEZ	Special Economic Zones
SFO	Serious Fraud Office
SIPO	State Intellectual Property Office
SOE	State-Owned Enterprise
SSE	Shanghai Stock Exchange
SZSE	Shenzhen Stock Exchange
TI	Transparency International
TSB	Technology and Science Bureau
UCMT	Urban construction and maintenance tax
UKBA	UK Bribery Act
VAT	Value-added tax
Vs.	Versus
WFOE	Wholly Foreign Owned Enterprise
WIPO	World Intellectual Property Organization
WHT	Withholding tax
WTO	World Trade Organization
WWII	Second World War
Yr	Year

Contents

List of Figures

List of Tables

List of Graphs

List of Contributors

Part 1: China 2.0—The New Stage
Stephen Green, Standard Chartered Bank
Binzhen Wu, Tsinghua University
Jim Rogers, Investment Expert
Dr. Stephen Dyer, A.T. Kearney
Dr. Daniel Zisper, McKinsey & Company, China

Part 2: Challenges
Chris Torrens, Control Risks
Belinda Tan, Deloitte

Part 3: Doing Business
Titus von dem Bongart, Ernst and Young
Sheng Tantzscher, Ernst and Young
Elliot Papageorgiou, Rouse Legal
Nandani Lynton, CEIBS University
Hanno D. Wentzler and Bettina Schoen, Freudenberg Group
Bryant J. Eggett, Mercer Consulting
Joerg Wuttke, BASF China

Part 4: The Chinese Way
Arnaud Debane, Superbrands

Introduction

A new era of increasing competition and complexity is emerging for companies doing business in China. For years, a seemingly endless supply of cheap labor helped China become the manufacturing powerhouse of the world and flooded global markets with its low-cost products. The major challenges for Western companies that operated in China during this time were the cultural and regulatory environment and a shortage of skilled workers. China's recent economic slowdown, however, indicates that this period is rapidly coming to an end.

China is entering a new stage of economic and societal development which we call *China 2.0*. This stage will be characterized by China's diminishing low-cost advantages due to sharply rising input costs and increased competition by local Chinese firms that have improved their quality and, in some cases, even begun to innovate.

In addition to higher costs and increased competition, societal factors will have a greater impact on how business is done in the *China 2.0* era, making it more complex to operate within the country. The People's Republic of China (PRC) has developed into a state full of contradictions. Economic liberalization has unleashed the entrepreneurship of the Chinese people, but the government still controls most of the economy through state-owned enterprises. Megacities on the east coast reveal breathtaking skylines, while western rural areas still resemble a third-world country. There are more luxury cars sold in China than in any other country in the world, yet more than 150 million people still live below the poverty line, with wages less than $1.25 US per day. *China 2.0* may prove painful for those managers and Western companies that are not prepared for this new reality. Businesses that are slow to adapt will struggle to remain successful or could even be forced to shut down their operations. Succeeding in the *China 2.0* era will require managers to reposition and reorganize their businesses, a process that needs to be based on a thorough reassessment of our current knowledge. This is especially true with regard to China, which, due to its rapid development, is already a much different country than it was portrayed to be only a few years ago.

CHINA BUSINESS 2.0 is intended to assist you in updating your knowledge in these areas and be your foundation for building an effective business strategy to capitalize on China's new development stage. This book covers more than 40 topics from an executive's perspective to help you conduct business in China in the future. Shaped by the experience we gained as expats who lived in the country for several years, we compiled information that gives you a solid economic background, explains how to comply with regulations and how to manage tasks, and helps you understand key cultural and social issues. CHINA BUSINESS 2.0 describes the status quo, draws your attention to new trends that will shape the future, and highlights areas where further reform will be unavoidable as the country moves forward.

To enhance practicality, CHINA BUSINESS 2.0 presents each topic in a short, easy-to-understand manner. We have also added numerous concise **'tips'**, **'opportunities'**, and **'warnings'** in separate boxes and **'suggestions for further reading'** at the end of several chapters.

CHINA BUSINESS 2.0 is broken down into four main parts:

1. **'China 2.0—The New Stage'** assesses the current status and future prospects of the Chinese economy, such as fundamental macroeconomic trends
2. **'Challenges'** focuses on the major difficulties China is facing in entering the next stage of development. It describes the status quo and its consequences in regard to dimensions like infrastructure, middle class, or innovation
3. **'Doing Business'** highlights important aspects that impact the execution of tasks when operating in the PRC. The topics in this section range from policy-related issues such as setting up legal entities, taxes, and Intellectual Property Rights to Human Resource management
4. **'The Chinese Way'** provides an overview of the unique cultural origins and the evolution of the administrative landscape while exploring their effects on business. This part of the book features topics such as historical influences, political forces, and social concepts with multiple tips and hands-on advice

Each part consists of various subchapters. Even though there are logical links between all the subchapters within each part, every topic can be read independently.

Throughout the book you will also find **'insight' sections** in which professionals and specialists in different domains share their experiences and opinions on the future trends of highly important topics. All of these experts have lived in China or have had major exposure to the country and possess real on-the-ground experience. Please note that these 'Insights' sections solely represent the opinions of these experts and have not been edited by the authors.

We all know that it is impossible to estimate future development in China. Whether you are simply trading goods with Chinese partners, managing a subsidiary, seeking an investment opportunity, or conducting a merger and acquisition, we sincerely hope that CHINA BUSINESS 2.0 gives you the background knowledge to identify major trends and find the right approach to the Chinese market for business success in this country.

Part I

China 2.0: The New Stage

"It does not matter what color a cat is, as long as it catches mice". This famous quote by Deng Xiao Ping very much illustrates how the Chinese leadership has changed its emphasis on the economic setup from the communist ideology to a competitive environment. The result of these changes has been seen during the past three decades. The PRC has reinvented its economy at a breathtaking pace, as it is now the world's second largest economy.

This part begins with an introduction on China's economic development stages and the changes we expect in the new *China 2.0* era. It also describes the economic fundamentals of the self-proclaimed "social market economy". The following chapters introduce topics of high economic importance in the PRC's new development stage. We describe the economic realities and trends, as well as indicate areas where the policy makers need to initiate further reforms. These are aspects you need to be aware of when doing business in this new *China 2.0* era.

In this part you will also gain insights on important regional differences which are sometimes overlooked, as the country has been unified under a centralized administration for centuries. However, these significant differences should always be considered when doing business in China.

China 2.0

1

China transformed from a peasant society to the world's second largest global economy within a single generation. With the opening of the economy and market reforms, entrepreneurial spirit has flourished: State-Owned Enterprises (SOEs) have been privatized, millions of Chinese have started new ventures, and China has taken advantage of its large labor force through low-cost manufacturing. But the PRC has come to a crucial juncture in its economic and social development. The current growth model is unbalanced towards exports and not sustainable in an environment of rising input costs. Thus, China's growth in the next decade will depend on the country's ability to move to the next stage of production through innovation and enhanced productivity and higher consumption through social stability (Fig. 1.1).

1.1 Reform Via a Step-by-Step Approach

In order to maintain close control over this economic development, Chinese leadership first invoked a step-by-step approach to reforms, or as often summarized by the famous expression, "cross the river by feeling the stones". On a trial and error basis, special regions were chosen for reform. If the reforms worked, they would be applied to new areas; if they failed they would be abandoned. This approach continues to this day.

The first economic changes, begun in the late 1970s, consisted of agricultural decollectivization by dismantling rural communes and giving entrepreneurs permission to start up businesses. Shortly thereafter, the area around Shenzhen (Guangdong province) was granted the status of a Special Economic Zone (SEZ) and thereby given favorable policies allowing for foreign trade and investments.

These reform approaches were almost instantly successful: China's agricultural production soared, and Shenzhen became an economic powerhouse. Consequently, other regions along the south-eastern seaboard were opened for foreign investment.

© Springer International Publishing Switzerland 2015

H.R. Randau, O. Medinskaya, *China Business 2.0*, Management for Professionals,
DOI 10.1007/978-3-319-07677-5_1

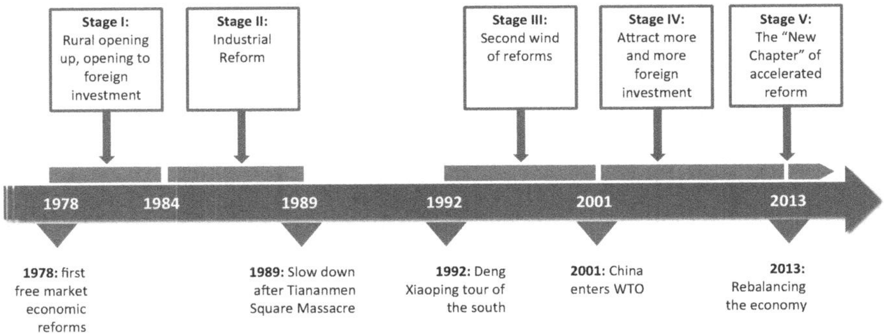

Fig. 1.1 Stages of economic development

In the beginning, foreign investments were mainly driven by Hong Kong (Yeung et al. 2009) while most industry remained state-owned.

The Tiananmen Square Massacre in 1989 caused a temporary slowdown in development, as debates about China's future direction ensued amongst leadership, but soon China continued its path towards further reform. Deng Xiaoping's southern tour of 1992 gave reforms a second wind and later that year China officially declared itself a "social market economy". Deng's crossing the river by feeling for stones approach allowed the government to gauge their local success before expanding to the nation at large. Leadership's primary objective for economic reform was to enhance political stability, so successful reforms were viewed as confirmation of the legitimacy of the Party's power and as a means of maintaining control. Thus, even though the share of State-Owned Enterprises shrank rapidly, leadership remained in control of strategic industries.

The 1990s saw economic growth accelerate at impressive annual double-digit rates.[1] The reform process moved from the south to interior provinces, Shanghai, and the Yangtze Delta.

In the 2000s, China's economic growth continued to soar, with GDP tripling between 2000 and 2010. China's acceptance into the World Trade Organization (WTO) in 2001 marked a new era for the country, opening the doors to foreign trade and accelerating the inflow of foreign investments. By 2003, China had become the biggest worldwide recipient of Foreign Direct Investments (FDIs). Business investments, particularly in industrial development and property, remained the most significant driver of growth.

[1] The World Bank (www.data.worldbank.org).

1.2 The New Stage

China's rapid economic growth has already affected nearly every aspect of daily life. But it has triggered also several economic and societal challenges. The export-heavy development has resulted in an unhealthy trade balance and low private consumption. Undoubtedly, China is on the verge of a new development stage, which we call *China 2.0*, a period in which the leadership needs to strengthen its efforts to rebalance the economy and society (Chap. 5).

The biggest challenge for the government and managers operating businesses in this China 2.0 era will be to respond to sharply increasing input costs. Labor, utility, land, and capital costs will continue to rise. Accordingly, Chinese businesses will need to boost productivity by investing in labor-substituting technologies if they intend to stay competitive. Achieving productivity gains will require a thorough analysis of current supply and value chains in regard to potential for atomization and digitization. Besides increased efficiency in manufacturing, managers will need to also place a higher focus on quality and the efficiency of back-office activities.

Currently, low-cost export business is getting more difficult and businesses are taking action to eliminate labor. This will eventually pose a major risk to the government, as it needs jobs to maintain political stability. Thus, it must be expected that the government focus will shift away from growth to job creation in the China 2.0 era. Generating new jobs will depend on the country's ability to move up the value chain and to innovate (Chap. 6) and boost household consumption.

Stimulating domestic demand, which declined from 46 % in 2000 to 34 % of GDP in 2012,[2] might prove especially difficult, given the complexity of societal problems that are driving consumer behavior. The previous decades have lifted hundreds of millions out of poverty and put them into a previously non-existent middle class (Chap. 7) in an increasingly urbanized society (Chap. 18). But the rapid growth has also created huge income disparities among individuals, (Chap. 19) as well as significant cross-regional inequalities (Chap. 3).

The government will have to embrace further fundamental structural reforms to unleash the Chinese consumption potential and close the large development gaps between regions and social classes. Recent developments indicate that China's leaders are ready to open a new chapter in their reform agenda, for example, in regard to the household registration system (Chap. 29) and a land rights reform (Chap. 17). Such reforms would have huge effects on the lives of the rural population, migration movements (Chap. 18), and income distribution (Chap. 19).

The Chinese leadership may also keep its promises to open more industries (e.g. electronic commerce or logistics) to foreign competitors. This would especially give western companies interesting business opportunities. But in the past the participation in such initiatives often required foreign companies to disclose their

[2] China Statistical Yearbook (www.stats.gov.cn/tjsj/ndsj/2013/indexeh.htm).

patents, technologies, and know-how. Accordingly, there was a high risk that such information would potentially be handed to Chinese competitors.

Other major issues on the political agenda in China 2.0 include the development of the Yuan as an international currency (Chap. 10), a high risk of non-performing loans (Chap. 8), and pressure on the labor market and the social welfare system (Chap. 20) by a rapidly aging society.

China 2.0 will also be shaped by the extensive use of new and advanced technologies. The focus will lie on headway in the use of alternative energy sources, more efficient use of energy, and intelligent transportation infrastructure. This will go hand in hand with an ongoing intensive use of electronic media. Chinese love to shop and chat via the Internet (Chap. 23). For businesses the major challenge will be to exploit these opportunities. The Chinese leadership will be challenged on how it manages to remain control over the political discussion and its ability to shape the public opinion as the Internet becomes more and more important in Chinese society.

INSIGHT: Stephen Green, Standard Chartered Bank

China's economic development and path forward

China's current investment-led growth model has a few more years to go but it is not sustainable. It is not going to collapse tomorrow, but there are clearly problems with it that have gotten worse in the past couple of years.

Today's Chinese economy is full of imbalances: between the east coast and the west, between investment and consumption, between the city and the countryside, and between rich and poor. The leadership tried to rebalance the economy by building an urban social welfare system through incentivizing manufacturing investment in western China, cutting taxes and boosting subsidies in rural areas, and encouraging rural-urban migration with some success.

The future challenges facing the economy, though, are more complex than these imbalances. China is facing at least four 'dynamic imbalances' today that are undermining the sustainability of growth and raising the risk of much slower growth and an economic crisis of some kind in the next decade. The 'dynamic imbalances' have the key characteristics of resulting in progressively worse inequality over time, and dynamic processes that previously 'worked' are now generating ever-bigger negative effects. These are namely the current urbanization process, the investment model, the relationship between government and the services economy and the government's role as both growth facilitator and interventionist.

Urbanization has generated growth as it raised the overall productivity of the workforce. However, the urbanization process also impoverishes the rural folks who lose their land, cannot afford to buy houses in urban areas, lack the skills to compete in the urban labor market, have their kids lose out on a good education, and because of *hukou* limitation have lost the social safety net. As a result inequality increases even as the economy urbanizes.

China's current investment model relies on high savings levels and subsidized credit via low interest rates. The costs for this model were acceptable as long as the financial system delivered growth. However, the costs are rising and the benefits are declining. Corporate and government balance sheets are now highly leveraged. This is the highest level ever; it is well above the 150%-of-GDP level reached in the early 2000s, the last time Beijing bailed out the banking system.

China has successfully produced a large urban middle class which now wants to buy quality services. They are concerned about food safety, corruption, health and education for their children- all things that the government, which is very efficient at taking land from farmers and building infrastructure , is not yet good at delivering. If the middle class remains dissatisfied, the risk rises that they leave the country, taking their talent and hard work with them.
In the past, China's large and powerful government sector was a facilitator for growth through infrastructure projects, granting subsidies to strategic sectors and preventing bankruptcies in a downturn. However, as society becomes wealthier and administrative powers are not curtailed, there are more opportunities for corruption. The other negative effect of an interventionist state is that the private sector gets hit. Entrepreneurs find it more difficult to start and operate businesses as the overall tax and fee rate is too high.

The solution to a dynamic imbalance is not a one-off policy change, but a re-engineering of the system so that positive outcomes are generated again. The coming round of reforms needs to focus on the 10- to 20-year horizon. The basic direction needs to be geared towards changing institutions which then help to grow into reform. As savings level drop over time and China urbanizes productivity will become more important than growth. Last but not least, competition needs to be allowed in as many fields as possible.

In practice this could mean that authorities may reform the migrant (*hukou*) system to support urbanization. The fair development of the corporate sector could be supported e.g. by checking the efficiency of SOEs, easing the over-regulated private sector or restructuring the government with the aim to increase its effectiveness. It could also mean that the government will get more serious about tax collection (introduction of an inheritance and capital gain tax) or collect higher funds from SOE's to support the strategic reform agenda (education, health care). Or the government centralizes the spending fiscal revenues which is still largely in the hands of local governments and too often not routed into projects that matter from a national perspective.

No matter what major economic reforms will be conducted, the days of crossing the river looking for stones, as the old proverb goes, are over. In today's Chinese economy all issues that the nation is facing are interconnected. China needs a long-term plan and strategy that will get it across the river without getting stuck in the middle. Otherwise the interventionist state will become dominant again.

Suggestion for Further Reading

Lin, J. Y. (2012). *Demystifying the Chinese economy*. Cambridge: Cambridge University Press.	
Rein, S. (2012). *The end of cheap China: Economic and cultural trends that will disrupt the world*. Hoboken: Wiley.	
Walter, C. E., & Howie, F. J. T. (2011). *Red Capitalism: The fragile financial foundation of China's extraordinary rise*. Singapore: Wiley.	
China Daily	www.chinadaily.com.cn

Reference

Yeung, Y.-M., Lee, J., & Kee, G. (2009). China's special economic zones at 30. *Eurasian Geography and Economics, 50*(2), 222–240.

2 China's Maturing Economy

China has delivered many years of consecutive double digit growth. An endless supply of cheap labor has made it the manufacturing powerhouse of the world. However, its recent economic slowdown indicates that the potential of generating further growth through low-cost exports is coming to its end.

The following chapter explains the current structure of GDP and other important key indicators in order to familiarize you with the major facts and trends the nation faces in the new China 2.0 era.

2.1 GDP by Sector

China's growth has been driven by its strength in secondary industries such as manufacturing, mining and construction. The share of the primary sector (agriculture) among these has fallen steadily but is still high compared to other developed countries. The workforce will thus continue to transit towards industrial jobs. The tertiary (service) sector is growing steadily but still lags behind not just developed countries but also peer BRICS countries. It certainly still has great development potential but will require the government to set further standards and moreover to enforce them. To develop a service-driven economy China still has a long way to go in developing a better legal framework, raising the quality of workforce, enforcing intellectual property rights, implementing safety standards and a client-focused culture.

© Springer International Publishing Switzerland 2015

H.R. Randau, O. Medinskaya, *China Business 2.0*, Management for Professionals,
DOI 10.1007/978-3-319-07677-5_2

2.2 GDP by Origin

Private household consumption is low in China when compared with developed nations, but is also low compared to developing nations like Brazil. Major growth drivers in the past were investments in infrastructure, construction and manufacturing, which supported a disproportionate amount of the economy.

The Chinese government has recognized this unhealthy development and is aiming to stimulate private consumption as a catalyst for economic growth.

2.3 Productivity

China's economic reforms of market liberalization and privatization led to huge productivity gains. The early 1980s saw a rapid increase in agricultural productivity, followed by improvements in state-owned enterprise efficiency and accelerated productivity as foreign direct investment started to pour into the country in the 1990s.

In absolute terms, China's productivity (measured in Total Factor Productivity (FTP), the change in output relative to change in labor and capital) remains comparatively low relative to western economies. There are multiple reason for this: as described China's economic growth still mainly depends on traditional technologies and sectors with a low added value. The country's agricultural mechanization is still at a relatively low level. State-owned enterprises, which play a major part in the economy, remain inefficient as they often concentrate on fulfilling social policy rather than striving for competitiveness. Last but not least the massive FDI inflows in past years concentrated mainly on the low value-added but labor-intensive manufacturing sector with only limited new or advanced technologies.

China still has great potential to increase productivity, especially in regards of labor and resource efficiency. The leadership is aware that it needs to take action to further support its productivity growth. Doing so will demand for further structural reforms to intensify competition (by opening up protected sectors), additional efforts to increase innovation and advanced technology or the use of ODI investments to import technologies and knowledge (Graphs 2.1 and 2.2, Table 2.1).

TIPS, OPPORTUNITIES, and WARNINGS

Warning: Statistics tend to be unreliable

"Official" Chinese government statistics can be unreliable. The government struggles to collect quality data because data recording is at times filed by self-interested parties, such as local authorities trying to provide positive economic figures to the party.

Experience has proved that if numbers look odd, they probably are off. Many experts therefore resort to other sources in case they feel numbers are not reliable.

Tip: Use alternative proxies

One of the most commonly used proxies for GDP development is electricity generation because, similar to energy consumption, a handful of big companies dominate the industry and report data directly to Beijing. Proxies for infrastructure and property are usually the cement and steel industries. Cement is perhaps the better proxy, as it is difficult to store and transport, and thus needs to respond quickly to changes in demand. Other experts use traffic data as a proxy, e.g. freight traffic, which has the advantage that there is little political reason to fake the data.

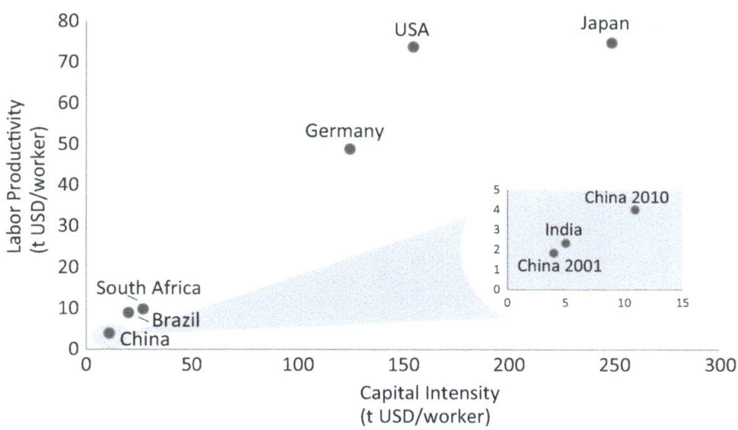

Graph 2.1 China's productivity. *Source*: Ernst and Young analysis (used with kind permission from Ernst and Young)

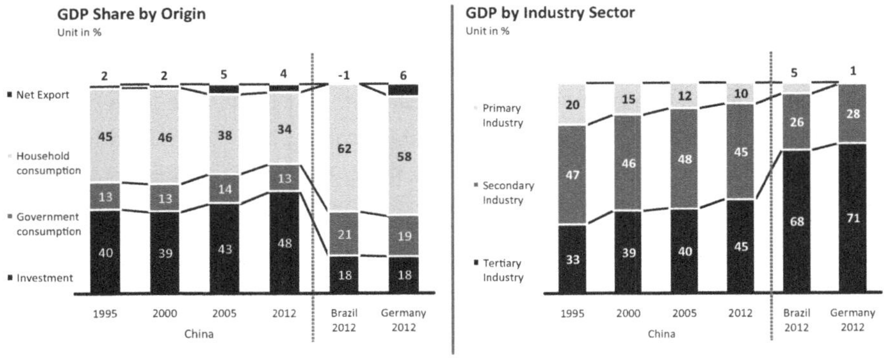

Graph 2.2 GDP by sector. *Source*: China Statistics Yearbook 2013, World Bank (used with kind permission from McKinsey & Company)

Table 2.1 Key economic metrics

		1995	2000	2005	2013
1. GDP	Billion US$	728	1,198	2,257	9,250
China's GDP, comprising approx. 10 % of the world economy, makes them the second largest economy in the world. China is expected to surpass the U.S. as the world's largest economy by 2020					
2. GDP per capita	US$	604	949	1,731	6,832
Despite China's high GDP, the average economic output per person is still low. The Chinese standard of living today is comparable to that of Japan in the 1950s and Taiwan and South Korea in the 1970s					
3. GDP development	% change on PY	10.9	8.4	11.3	7.7
Over the past 20 years, the Chinese economy has grown quickly and steadily, with rising activity in most of the economy, particularly in fixed investments					
4. Inflation rate	% change on PY	16.9	0.3	1.8	2.57
From 1994 until 2010, the average inflation rate in China was 4.25 %, reaching a historical high of 27.7 % in October of 1994 and a record low of −2.2 % in March of 1999. The major concern for the Chinese populace is that food prices may rise faster than core inflation					
5. FDI net	Billion US$	36	38	117	118
China is the largest receiver of FDI in the world, due to its relatively low costs of production, increasingly modernized infrastructure and productive means, and 'untapped' markets in many consumer-based industries (Buckley 2010)					
6. Unemployment rate	% of total labor force	2.9	3.1	4.2	4.1
In 2012, there were approx. nine million unemployed urban citizens. Since official statistics generally represent citizens registered with the Ministry of Labor in urban areas, unemployment rates are often underestimated, if not sometimes virtually meaningless. By including unemployed migrants, unemployed citizens in rural areas, and part time workers unable to obtain full-time positions, this figure could be 9–10 % higher					
7. Gross domestic savings	% of GDP	43.5	37.5	47.6	51[a]
China's high rate of savings is attributable to citizens' concerns about the social safety net (health care, retirement), low household incomes, and the structural focus on investment. However, the government is trying to encourage consumption in lieu of saving in order to contribute to GDP growth					
8. Budget balance	% of GDP	−1.7	−2.5	−0.3	−1.9
The central government's budget has been steadily increasing. Major expenditures include military, education, social safety and employment, and science and technology					
9. Net foreign assets	Billion US$	75.4	165.6	818.9	1,737.3[a]
China holds the largest amount of foreign exchange reserves in the world (3.7 trillion US$ in 2013)[b]. About 60 % of the reserves consist of U.S. dollars. China holds these large sums of foreign reserves as a means of stabilizing the RMB exchange rate and avoiding upwards revaluation					
10. Military spending	Billion US$	20.9	33.5	64.7	166
China's 2013 military budget is the second largest in the world[c]. Military expenditures have increased exponentially in recent years (and will continue to grow rapidly) but still lag well behind the U.S. which spends more than four times as much. In terms of sheer personnel, however, the Chinese military has by far the greatest number					

1, 3, 6, 8 Xinhua; 2 World Economic Outlook Database-April 2013, International Monetary Fund; 4 www.inflation.eu; 5,7 Worldbank; 9 Peterson Institute for International economics: China Economic Watch (www.piie.com); 10 SIPRI Military Expenditure Database, 2013

[a]Data from 2012

[b]Wall Street Journal (www.online.wsj.com)

[c]Stockholm International Peace Research Institute (www.sipri.org)

INSIGHT: Binzhen Wu, Tsinghua University

The reasons behind China's high savings rate

China's high savings rate may harm future economic development because it limits consumption.

Certainly, the foremost reason for Chinese to save large amounts of their disposable income is the weak social security network. The latest expansion of social programs (health care, retirement) shows no effect on the rate, although it may have consequences in the future. Thekey question will be how the expansion is financed. If the expansion is financed by raising income taxes, it may even reduce consumption in the future.

A second reason is that migrant workers tend to save large amounts of their salaries, because of low social protection due to the *hukou* system (Chap. 29). Having only very limited access to welfare benefits when they live in urban areas forces them to save far more of their income than holders of urban *hukou*.

One may also assume that high housing prices (Chap. 17) have led to a higher savings rate. But recent studies find no evidence for that assumption.

Gender roles would be a third reason for ahigh household savings rate. Tradition expects young men to buy an apartment before marriage. Since the share of households with male children tends to be higher in Chinese society (Chap. 15), there is an even greater incentive to save in households with boys than in households with girls.

However, rising income inequality has begun to shift the saving attitude towards greater spending. Today financial hurdles to changing social status and moving up within society tend to be higher,requiring a stronger financial investment in education,housing, or luxury items

2.4 Inward Foreign Direct Investment

Inward FDI has been a major driver of China's economic rise. Driven by a depreciating U.S. dollar and the liberalization of trade by planned economies, the World FDI started to take off by the end of the 1980s. China benefited greatly from this trend. The decision by PRC leaders to make FDI part of the national development strategy has proven successful. A huge surplus of cheap labor (in 1990 roughly 850m Chinese or approx. 75 % of the total population lived in rural areas), a large market and favorable policy led to high growth rates of FDI inflows. China has received the most inward FDI in the developing world for more than two decades. Inward FDI first surged after Deng Xiaoping toured Guangdong and Shanghai in early 1992, followed by a second wave after the country joined the World Trade Organization in 2001.

Inward FDI helped to develop the country's industrial base, promoted regional development, boosted employment, transferred technology and increased exports. Historically these investments were directed mainly to the labor-intensive manufacturing industry on the east coast. In recent years the growth rate of FDI inflow has slowed down due to sharply rising wages, a declining workforce and increased urbanization. Cost considerations may mean that more Western locations will be a target of inflowing investments, or international investors will look for alternative FDI destinations in Asia.

The growth of inward FDIs into manufacturing has already decelerated while that into service-oriented sectors has accelerated—a trend which most likely is going to continue. With half of its total population now in urban areas and the manufacturing sector losing competitiveness due to sharply rising costs (both wage growth and currency appreciation), China's growth in the next decade will depend on the country's ability to move to the next stage of production and consumption. Its rising middle class and increasingly urbanized society mean that FDI will be increasingly aimed at serving the domestic market rather than taking advantage of low costs. This is already happening: FDI inflows into the manufacturing sector have decelerated while those into service-oriented sectors have accelerated. FDI inflows in the manufacturing sector contracted, reflecting the structural adjustment of labor-intensive FDI shifting to other Asian countries (Nguyen 2013).

2.5 Outward Foreign Direct Investment

Non-financial outbound foreign investment was 90 billion US$ in 2013,[1] surging from as low as just 0.9 billion US$ in 2000.[2] Outgoing FDIs were only around half of incoming FDIs for most past years, with investments in Hong Kong accounting for close to 2/3 (much of the investment first passes through Hong Kong en route to other destinations).[3]

China's approach to overseas takeovers has changed significantly. After the government first permitted local companies to make acquisitions abroad in the early 2000s, companies suddenly began concentrating on takeovers to gain market

[1] Reuters (www.reuters.com).

[2] UNCTADstat (unctad.org).

[3] *China gets serious about ODI*, 01.12.2011, can be found at: www.forbes.com

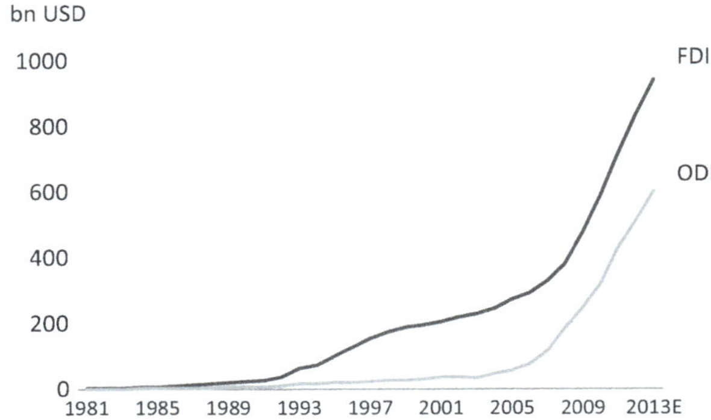

Fig. 2.1 China global FDI vs. ODI stock. *Source*: UNCTADstat

share abroad. But many of these initial takeovers ended in utter failure, with Chinese companies having to abort them or sell off their acquisitions. The government seems to have changed its course by encouraging Chinese companies to purchase physical assets rather than intangible ones (Fig. 2.1).

China's outgoing FDI is expected to grow in the upcoming years as China seeks outlets for its foreign exchange reserves. Outward FDI may even surpass incoming FDI in the next 5 years as the Ministry of Commerce encourages domestic companies to invest overseas. Chinese companies are seeking diverse foreign investment opportunities, including both raw material based emerging markets and mature, high technology developed markets. Such investments are now directed towards strengthening the domestic Chinese market position rather than gaining foreign market space. Without a doubt it will remain an important cornerstone in the country's quest towards higher innovation because it will give Chinese companies the chance to gain experience and import advanced technologies.

TIPS, OPPORTUNITIES and WARNINGS

Warning: Financial transactions are often routed through Hong Kong

Any analysis of China's FDI situation needs to include the development in Hong Kong, as it takes a central role in channeling funds to and from mainland China.

Suggestions for Further Reading

CEIC Data: a Product of ISI Emerging Markets	www.ceicdata.com
China Statistical Yearbook	www.stats.gov.cn
General Administration of Customs of China	www.english.customs.gov.cn
The Heritage Foundation: China Global Investment Tracker	www.heritage.org/research/projects/china-global-investment-tracker-interactive-map
The Economist	www.economist.com
The Economist Intelligence Unit	www.eiu.com
The World Bank Database	www.data.worldbank.org
United States Census Bureau	www.census.gov
UNCTADstat	www.unctad.org
U.S.–China Economic and Security Review Commission	www.uscc.gov
United Nations Conference on Trade and Development	www.unctadstat.unctad.org/EN/
Buckley, P. J. (2010). *Foreign direct investment, China and the world economy*. Houndmills: Palgrave Macmillan.	

References

Buckley, P. J. (2010). *Foreign direct investment: China and the world economy*. Houndmills: Palgrave Macmillan.

Nguyen, T. D. (2013). *The great migration. How FDI is moving to ASEAN and India*. Hong Kong: HSBC Global Research.

3 The Economic Landscape

3.1 Significant Economic Differences Between Regions

China has been united for many centuries, but its provinces reveal significant differences in language, tastes in food, fashion, and purchasing power. China's regions also manifest huge differences in their industrial focus. This can, in many ways, be attributed to the active government promotion of a specific industry, even to the extent that the entire vertical supply chains of these industries are located in such regions. Accordingly, a 'One China' company policy cannot be successful in a China 2.0 environment. Instead, managers will have to respond to local tastes through localized marketing, product development, and services.

3.2 Geographical Areas

China's economy can be split into four geographical areas: northeastern China along the coastline of the Yellow Sea, the Yangtze River delta, the Pearl River delta, and Central and western China, which stretches to the Sichuan basin and the mountainous, rough landscape of Tibet and the Himalayas (Fig. 3.1).

The eastern coastline, where reforms were first introduced, is the most populated and one of the densest regions in the world. Occupying approximately 10 % of China's territory, it is China's economic powerhouse, sporting many fine harbors, big cities, and an excellent, well-developed infrastructure. The wealth disparity between the east coast and the rest of China, significant since the onset of reforms, has only widened in the past 30 years. As China has developed, foreign investors have constantly looked towards this eastern region, bolstering its economic power. Today, some eastern provinces have reached the economic capacity of entire well-developed countries such as Switzerland and Finland (Fig. 3.2).

The economic landscape, however, is starting to shift. Due to the discrepancy between China's east and west economies, the government launched the so called "Go West" initiatives in the late 1990s. In order to balance inequalities, these

© Springer International Publishing Switzerland 2015

H.R. Randau, O. Medinskaya, *China Business 2.0*, Management for Professionals,
DOI 10.1007/978-3-319-07677-5_3

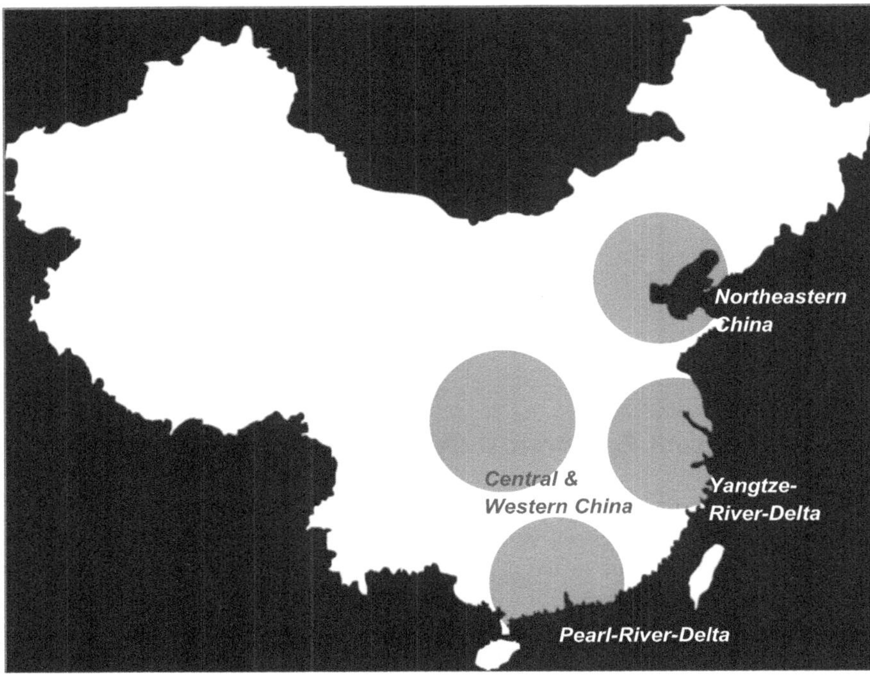

Fig. 3.1 Regional economic hubs

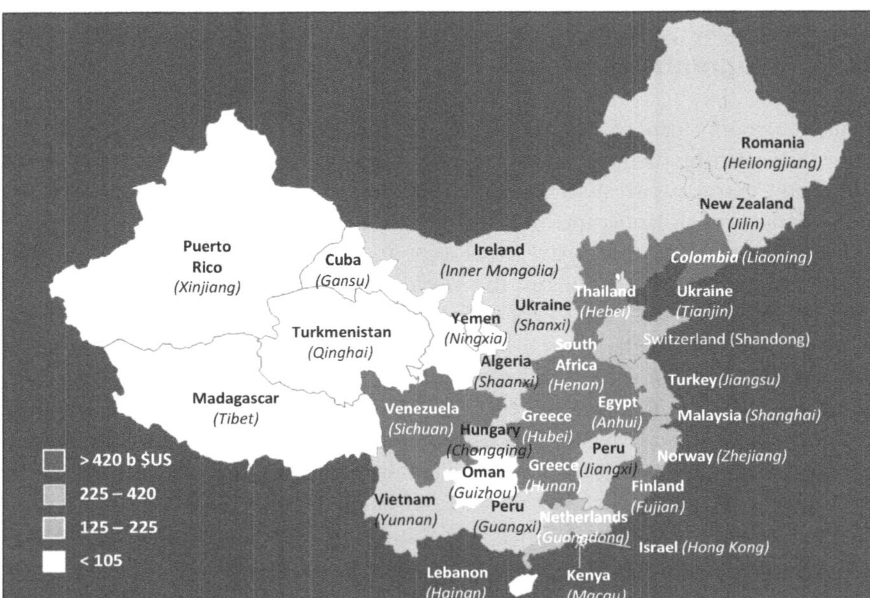

Fig. 3.2 GDP (nominal) for regions with countries equivalents 2012. *Source*: Own representation with data from Statistical Year Book China, CIA (idea based on http://www.economist.com/content/chinese_equivalents)

policies heavily incentivize growth in Central and western China. Because of "Go West", together with saturated markets and sharply increasing labor costs in the east, growth in the west has already been considerable. But since education, infrastructure, and general human capital in the region is remains largely underdeveloped, speedy development in the west could be challenging.

3.3 Northeastern China

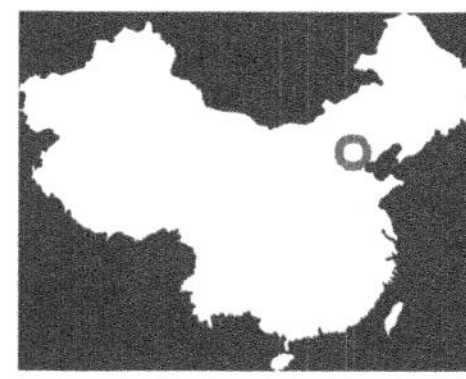

Northeast China is the country's traditional industrial base, focusing mainly on equipment manufacturing. Major industries include steel, automobile, chemicals, textile, shipbuilding, aircraft manufacturing, and petroleum refining.

Beijing, or Peking, is China's capital and political, educational, and cultural center. It houses all the important national, governmental, and political institutions, including the National People's Congress.

Tianjin, located only 112 km from Beijing, is a quickly developing area (GDP +30 % p.a.) and a base of innovation—especially in aerospace, aviation, petrochemicals, and alternative energy. Tianjin's port has China's biggest container terminal.

Located on the northeast coast, **Dalian** is an important harbor city. The city is the gateway to Beijing and Tianjin, handling 80 % of the export cargos from the region.

3.4 The Yangtze River Delta

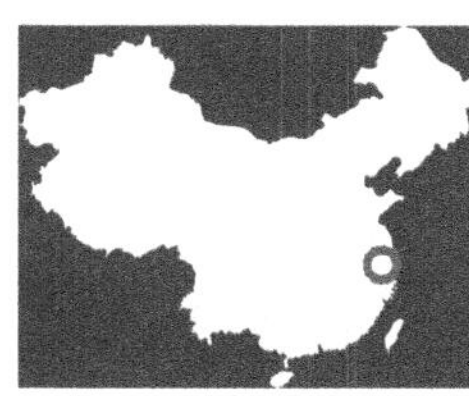

This region, which includes the municipality of Shanghai and the provinces of Jiangsu and Zhejiang, is China's second most economically powerful region. The region a large manufacturing base, and is also known for hi-tech and biotech products. Besides Shanghai, its most important cities are Nanjing, Suzhou (Jiangsu province), Hangzhou and Ningbo (Zhejiang province).

Shanghai is China's most populous urban area, and the showpiece of China's economy. Today, Shanghai has achieved a global status as one of the world's premier international hubs. According to the standardized Globalization and World Cities ranking, Shanghai holds an Alpha+rating, signifying it as one of the world's ten most important service centers. The city's three largest service industries are retail, real estate, and financial services, and with the world's largest container port, Shanghai hopes to be an international shipping center in the near future.

TIPS, OPPORTUNITIES and WARNINGS

Opportunity: Shanghai's new free-trade zone

Shanghai's new free-trade zone is nearly an 11-sq mile district that covers four existing special trade zones in the Pudong district. Selected to offer new financial services, it might provide possibilities to establish new business models previously not allowed in Mainland China. It will be interesting to see how it develops, as it most likely will serve as a testing ground for financial experiments before it is attempted elsewhere in China.

Warning: Pay attention to local differences

Many western companies' offices are located on China's East coast, specifically in Shanghai and Beijing. This being the case, they need to localize marketing and all types of product development, keeping in mind regional standards and behavior.

3.5 The Pearl River Delta

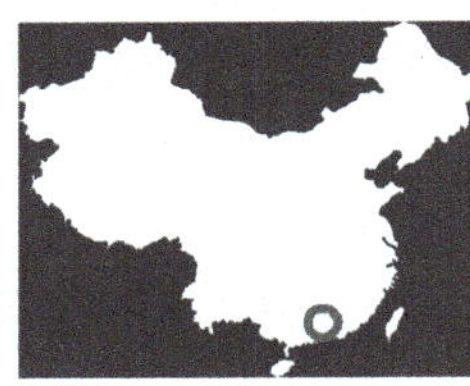

Located in Guangdong Province in the south, the Pearl River Delta is the country's most prosperous region and its technology manufacturing heartland. The region was the first part of the country opened up to foreign investment. Its proximity to Hong Kong has made the region a key export and production center ever since China's first economic reforms in the late 1970s. The region's economy is largely driven by manufacturing—especially in cheap electronics, toys, and garments.

Guangzhou (also called Canton) is the third largest city in China and the capital of Guangdong Province. It is close to the South China Sea and the cities of Hong Kong and Macau. The city is a major trading port and the industrial and business center of southern China.

Shenzhen is famous for being China's first Special Economic Zone opened to foreign trade in 1980. Chinese and foreign companies have heavily invested in Shenzhen's economy and have spurred its incredible growth and development. The city also houses the Shenzhen Stock Exchange.

3.6 Central and Western China

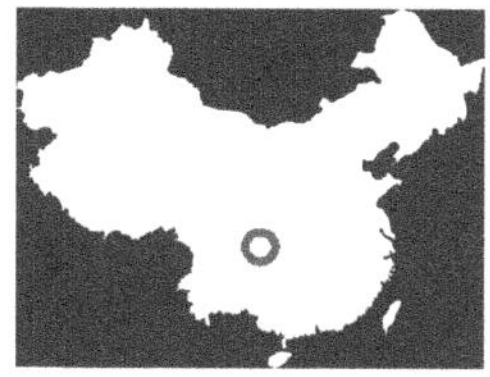

"Go West" policies, which will continue until at least 2020, promote tax breaks and investment benefits for business development in this region. Along with low labor costs, this has led to noticeable growth in cities such as Chengdu, Chongqing, and Wuhan.

Chengdu, the booming capital of Sichuan Province, is a rapidly growing economic center featuring light and heavy manufacturing, aluminum smelting, chemicals, electronics and information technology industries. The city's industrial development zone has attracted many multinationals, especially those from the growing automotive sector. Though the city still lacks the prowess of the coastal areas, its growth potential remains very large.

The official municipality of **Chongqing** is technically the most populous in China, with 32 million inhabitants under direct municipal control. Its urban population, though, is only 6 or 7 million. Chongqing was once part of Sichuan Province, but was made its own administrative body in 1997, in effort to kick start the "Go West" strategy. Chongqing has become a major manufacturing center (automobile, chemical, pharmaceuticals, processing), is China's third largest center of motor vehicle production, and is its largest center for motorcycles. Chongqing is also supporting increasing numbers of multinational corporations.

Capital of Hubei Province, **Wuhan** is one of Asia's most progressive business cities. It is a natural hub for transportation due to its ideal location at the confluence of the Han and Yangzi rivers. The government therefore hopes to make Wuhan the center's economic growth engine.

3.7 Special Administrative Regions

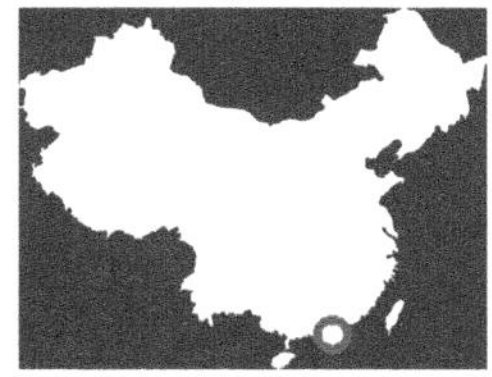

Hong Kong was a British colony from 1842 to 1997 and with its handover it became China's first Special Administrative Region (SAR). Nowadays, Hong Kong is one of the world's leading international financial centers, characterized by a capitalist economic system with low taxation and free trade, which has helped make the Hong Kong dollar one of the most traded currencies in the world. It is one of the most densely populated areas on the globe, and is often described as a place where "east meets west".

Macau was a Portuguese colony until its handover in 1999 and its economy is strongly focused on gambling and tourism.

Suggestions for Further Reading

All China Data Center: China Provincial Statistical Yearbooks	www.chinadataonline.org
Business in China Factbook	www.ec.europa.eu/trade/policy/countries-and-regions/countries/china/
China Daily	www.chinadaily.com.cn
Guo, R. (2013). *Regional China: A business and economic handbook*. New York: Routledge.	
South China Morning Post	www.scmp.com
The Economist	www.economist.com

4 Domination of State-Owned Enterprises

China runs a bifurcated economy. While a robust and competitive private sector dominates industries like clothing, food, and factory-assembled exports, sectors of strategic importance such as railways, financial services, utilities, energy, telecommunications, education services, and health care are generally not open to private investment. These protected sectors are extensively controlled through government interventions and often dominated by large SOEs.

The 1990s saw big changes for SOEs, as the government forced companies not making a profit to either merge into larger corporations or to file bankruptcy. Many of these remaining SOEs have since become private companies. They have emerged as modern, restructured, share-holding firms listed on the domestic stock market. But even though the Chinese government has legally separated itself from these companies or sold a minority of their shares, either the state or local governments or SOEs often retain the majority of the shares.

The Chinese National Bureau of Statistics uses a very strict definition and views SOEs as only those economic units where 100 % of the shares are owned by the state. The most important of these SOEs (currently 117 corporations[1]) report directly to a special commission under the State Council called the Assets Supervision and Administration Commission of the State Council (SASAC). Accordingly, they are obliged to coordinate their investments and the appointment of top management positions with the SASAC. But realistically, SOEs that have transitioned to private companies should also be seen as SOEs because the government has never relaxed its control over these companies. Using a broader definition such as this shows that approximately 40 % of China's GDP is generated by SOEs or entities directly controlled by SOEs.[2] Not surprisingly, all but one of the

[1] According to State-owned Assets Supervision and Administration Commission of the State Council (SASAC) in 2013.

[2] US-China Economic and Security Review Commission (www.uscc.gov).

© Springer International Publishing Switzerland 2015

H.R. Randau, O. Medinskaya, *China Business 2.0*, Management for Professionals,
DOI 10.1007/978-3-319-07677-5_4

Table 4.1 Ten largest state-owned enterprises (Fortune 500 List 2013)

Company name	Revenue (billion US$)
1. China Petroleum and Chemical Corporation	428
2. China National Petroleum Corporation	409
3. State Grid Corporation of China	289
4. Industrial and Commercial Bank of China	133
5. China Construction Bank Corporation	113
6. Agricultural Bank of China	104
7. Bank of China	98
8. China Mobile Communication Corporation	97
9. China State Construction Engineering	91
10. China National Offshore Oil	84

Source: Fortune Global 500

100 largest publicly-listed Chinese companies have a majority of their shares owned by the state (Table 4.1).

Even though the government might be forced to gradually open some protected sectors in the future in order to increase productivity through intensified competition, the Chinese leaders will continue to protect and support SOEs in fields of strategic importance, as well as tightly control sectors of strategic importance such as technology, natural resources, energy, and transportation. State-controlled companies are significant in reaching ambitious goals, such as promoting technological progress or ensuring national security, e.g. by securing work places.

In general, SOEs often receive preferential treatment in various forms. The central and especially local governments, provide favorable loans and subsidies and set regulations that tend to benefit these companies. Thus, some SOEs have grown rapidly and rank among the world's largest companies. In 2012, 60[3] Chinese SOEs were listed in the Fortune Global 500, including three of the Top Ten.[4] The minority shareholders usually receive only a small portion of the profits, as SOEs tend to pay few dividends. The earnings are mostly collected by the *SASAC* and reinvested in SOEs under their supervision, adding only little to boost household consumption.

But the problem remains that many SOEs are often inefficient and inflexible. They also tend to deliver low return on investment ratios as they are often used to achieve certain social policy goals. Their success often stems from regulatory protection and the fact that they are supported by their very large home markets rather than operational excellence. Even though they have made vast progress, many SOEs still need to improve their professionalism and internationalization in order to truly be able to compete with western multinationals.

[3] South China Morning Post (www.scmp.com).

[4] Fortune Global 500: Our annual ranking of the world's largest corporations (http://money.cnn.com).

Initiating change within the SOEs will most likely also require them to change their governance models in the future. China's leaders have admired Singapore's success as early as their own reform days in the late 1970s. The Singaporean governance model with a strong investment holding could serve as a blueprint for China's future. Companies that are owned under Singapore's state holding investment umbrella are known as "government-linked companies" (GLDs). The Singaporean government avoids getting involved in the day-to-day business. Instead, GLDs are run by professional managers. Currently, it is difficult to imagine that Chinese leaders would retreat to having only the role of an active investor with limited direct influence. But reform in a similar direction seems to be unavoidable if China is serious about taking the next step on the economic ladder towards higher productivity, greater innovation, and stronger consumption.

TIPS, OPPORTUNITIES and WARNINGS

Warning: SOEs are protected from competition

Even though the government might be forced to gradually open some protected sectors in the future in order to increase productivity through intensified competition, the Chinese leaders will continue to protect and support SOEs in fields of strategic importance.

Directly competing with SOEs may prove to be a risky strategy. They tend to benefit greatly from the various forms of preferential treatment they receive. This often effectively guarantees that an SOE will be a stronger player on the local market than all the other companies. You also need to consider that courts may also rule in favor of major local companies when they are in disputes with foreign firms, particularly when these firms have political affiliations or are major sources of employment or tax revenue.

Rebalancing the Economy: The 12th Five-Year Plan

5

China's overarching objective is a rebalancing of the economy—away from a unsustainable growth model that depends disproportionately on exports and capital investment towards greater domestic consumption. The shift is intended to solve social challenges including the rising income disparity, a weak social safety (welfare) net, and pollution, which pose a potential risks to the current order (Fig. 5.1).

The intended shift is mirrored by China's current Five Year Plan which was ratified by the National Congress in 2011 and is based on four key initiatives: restructuring the economy, promoting strategic industries and innovation, improving social welfare, and implementing energy-saving and environmental-protection measures (Fig. 5.2).[1]

5.1 Economic Restructuring

The government plans to slow the pace of GDP growth down by reducing its focus on fixed asset investment (FAI) and setting policies to slowly increase consumption from a very low level in the mid 30 % range of GDP in 2010 to 35 % in 2015. Measures to shift the growth pattern away from a model based on the dependency on exports and capital investment by increasing private consumption will include strong increases in minimum wages (averaging no less than double digits per year), a personal income tax reform, and expanded government-funded social welfare spending for health care and pensions. Alongside these initiatives, the service sector shall grow to account for close to 50 % of GDP in 2015.

[1] McKinsey Quarterly, *China's next chapter: China's great rebalancing: Promise and peril*, Yasheng Huang, 2013 Number 3, pp. 34–39; American Chamber Shanghai Insight, *China's 12th Five-Year Plan*, Kenneth Jarrett and Carly Ramsey, April 2011, can be found at: http://www.amcham-shanghai.org/amchamportal/infovault_library/2011/China's_12th_Five-Year_Plan.pdf

© Springer International Publishing Switzerland 2015

H.R. Randau, O. Medinskaya, *China Business 2.0*, Management for Professionals,
DOI 10.1007/978-3-319-07677-5_5

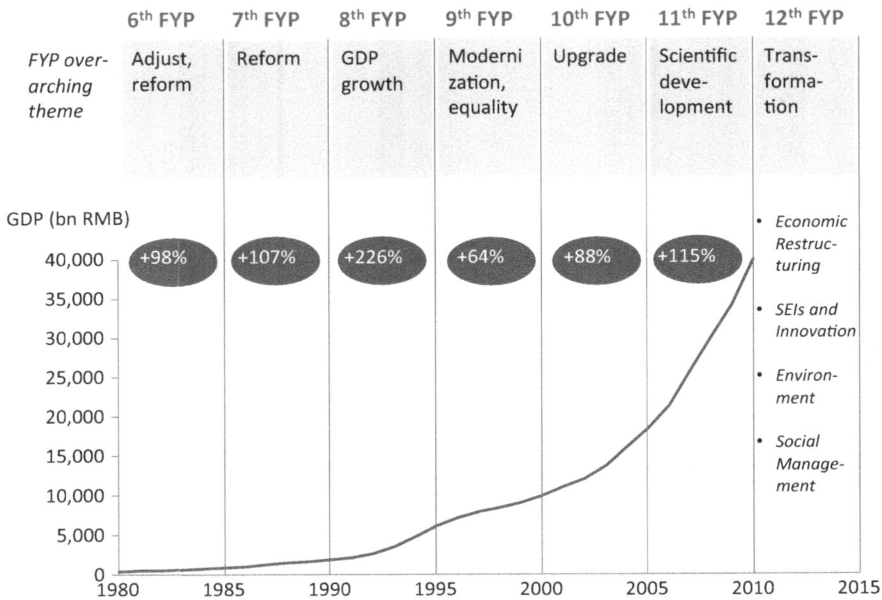

Fig. 5.1 Focus of Five-Year Plans and Effect on GDP. *Source*: Used with kind permission from McKinsey & Company

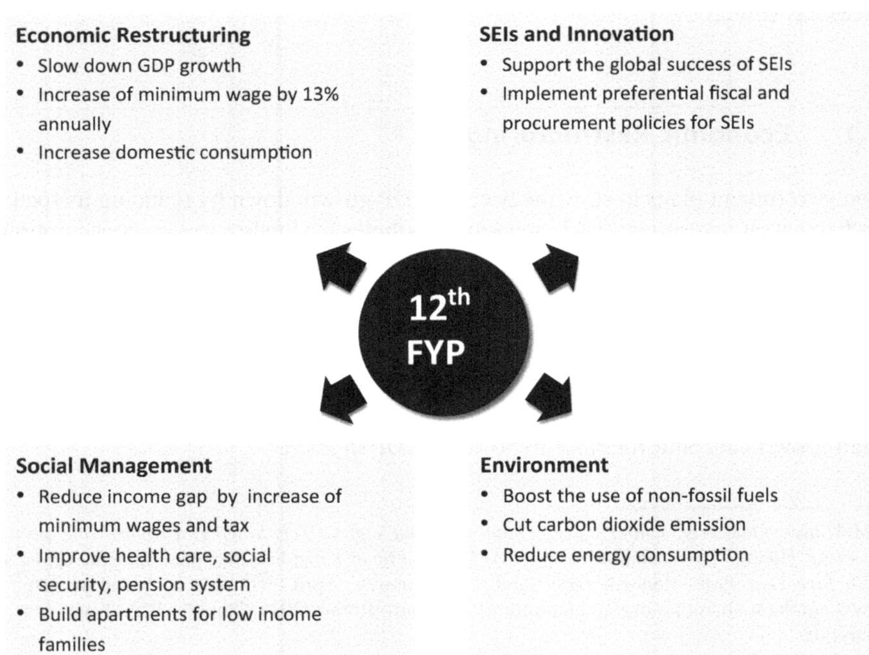

Fig. 5.2 Focus of China's 12th Five Year Plan

It must be stated that this element of the Five-Year-Plan could prove very challenging. Similar themes have been on the government agenda already in past five-year plans, to little avail. Enforcing a controlled GDP growth may be problematic, since central-level and local-level objectives are difficult to align. Local governments, particularly in western regions, may still strive for their own success by overachieving central-government targets and by taking advantage of their significant growth potential.

5.2 Strategic Industries and Innovation

China plans to boost several "Strategic Emerging Industries" (SEIs) which shall become the backbone of a restructured Chinese economy. The government hopes that Chinese corporations will succeed in these sectors on a global scale.

The seven SEIs are: biotechnology, new energy, high-end equipment manufacturing, energy conservation and environmental protection, clean energy vehicles, new materials, and next-generation information technology.

The government will spend as much as 14 trillion RMB on these industries through 2015 in an effort to increase the contribution of SEIs from today's approximately 5 % of GDP to 8 % by 2015. Further plans are to increase SEI contributions to 15 % of GDP by 2020. The government will likely release numerous preferential fiscal and procurement policies to develop these SEIs. Together with initiatives to enhance scientific and technological innovation, expenditures on research and development should reach 2.2 % of GDP by 2015.[2]

5.3 Social Equity

China aims to achieve a more equitable wealth distribution by raising minimum wages, adjusting individual income tax, and improving social infrastructure. According to the FYP, the government intends to accelerate the reform and development of healthcare, improve the coverage of social security systems for urban and rural residents, and provide pension schemes covering all rural residents and 357 million urban residents.[3] In addition, the government announced the construction and renovation of 36 million apartments for low-income families.

[2] Sano, Junya, Key Targets in the 12th Five-Year Plan and Policies for their Realization: Reasons for the 7 % Growth Target, in: RIM: Pacific Business and Industries, 2011.

[3] China pledges full coverage of pension system, 11.06.2012, can be found at: www.chinadaily.com

5.4 Environmental Initiatives

China has declared environmental goals and embedded several binding energy-efficiency targets in the FYP. These include boosting the proportion of non-fossil fuels in primary energy use from 8 % to 11.4 % and cutting carbon dioxide emissions by 17 % per unit of GDP. Even though these objectives are not overly ambitious, they reveal China's intention to develop a low-carbon economy while improving energy security.

INSIGHT: Jim Rogers, Beeline Investment

China's economic role in the 21st century

In my view, the 21st century is going to be the century of Asia with China being the dominant force. We live in a time with huge debt imbalances in the world. The debts are in the West (U.S. is the largest debtor) and the assets are in Asia (China being currently the largest creditor in the world). Those imbalances have to be resolved, and this process will lead to currency turmoil, inflation and even the fall of governments, like it frequently did in the past. Whenever there has been a global economic crisis, a new player has always emerged on the economic landscape. This time it could be China with its currency the Yuan. The nation has a recipe for a sound currency — a huge population, an enormous balance of payments surplus, and a sizeable GDP to match. For the moment, its currency is not convertible, but this must and will change in the coming years.

The Chinese nation has been extraordinarily successful several times in history, and it will happen again. It has a long tradition of entrepreneurship and capitalism (except the period from 1949 to 1978, when China's economy was essentially Socialist). It has embraced economic reform, rebuilding its infrastructure with speedy super highways and new construction everywhere. Chinese people save a large portion of their income which has formed the foundation of the country's economic development and leaves room for future consumption. In addition overseas Chinese have lots of capital and expertise which will fuel future growth.

In many regards China reminds me of the U.S. at the beginning of the 20th century. The U.S. at the time also displayed huge potentials. Certainly China's rise is not going to happen overnight or straight up. The nation will go through several ups and downs and face several serious economic setbacks over the coming years. Some parts of the economy will continue to boom while others will have a "hard landing". China's growth drivers will need to be evaluated carefully, and one will have to analyze where bubbles have developed. The real estate and property market is an obvious risk, and it is very difficult to guess the sector's future. China's environment is heavily polluted, and the nation will face tremendous costs in healthcare as its population ages rapidly. Corruption is still widespread even though we have seen significant improvements. Certainly the current, solely on manufacturing focused, business model is not sustainable. China will need to move up the value chain, and it remains to be seen whether it can fulfill its ambitious innovation targets.

But these risks also provide many opportunities. The current pollution e.g. means that in the next 10 to 15 years, the pollution control and environmental protection industry will have important development opportunities.

We need to be patient. In the long-run the country has whatever it takes to become a very successful nation. To observe China's economic development requires a deep understanding of its economic drivers as well as cultural and societal roots. In addition one will need to be able to understand and read Chinese. I advise everyone to invest time and effort to learn more about China, as its economic rise is going to change the world as we know it.

Suggestions for Further Reading

American Chamber Shanghai: Insight Magazine	www.amcham-shanghai.org
China Daily	www.chinadaily.com.cn
McKinsey Quarterly: China's next Chapter	www.mckinsey.com

Sano, J. (2011). *Key targets in the 12th five-year plan and policies for their realization: Reasons for the 7% growth target.* In RIM: Pacific Business and Industries.

Moving Forward: China's Plan to Innovation

6

One of key objectives of the 12th FYP is to transit the economy from "Made in China" to "Created in China".[1] As costs increase and the Yuan strengthens, moving up the value chain will be of utmost importance in balancing the export-driven economy and securing China's global competitiveness.

Progress is already visible: R&D spending and patent applications have risen significantly (although some critics attribute much of the latter to "junk" patents). China has already created the seeds of 22 Silicon Valley-like innovation hubs within the life sciences and biotech industries.[2] One of the most impressive of these lies in *Zhongguancun* in northwestern Beijing—an innovative hotspot populated with countless research centers, tech super-companies, and start-ups.

Leadership has set clear, but challenging targets, which may prove difficult to achieve: to spend 2.5 % of China's GDP on R&D by 2020; to be among the top five countries with regard to number of inventions patented; and to have Chinese-authored scientific papers among the world's most cited.[3] In contrast to the market based innovation approach of other countries, where R&D is encouraged by taxation benefits and the market determines the winning technology options, the Chinese government has taken an active role in allocating funding to specific industrial segments and technologies. It has implemented a range of policies to enhance innovation, including national level research programs, increased spending on education, and a so-called 'Thousand Talents' scheme which encourages scientists working overseas to return to China (Table 6.1).

To encourage an innovation-based economy, leadership has sought to reduce "foreign technology dependency" through 'indigenous innovation' policies.

[1] Wen Jiabao at the Fifth Session of the Eleventh National People's Congress on 05.03 2012 (http://english.gov.cn).

[2] *A CEO's guide to innovation in China*, 2012, can be found at: http://www.mckinseyquarterly.com

[3] The state's Science and Technology Development Plan.

© Springer International Publishing Switzerland 2015
H.R. Randau, O. Medinskaya, *China Business 2.0*, Management for Professionals,
DOI 10.1007/978-3-319-07677-5_6

Table 6.1 Comparison of innovation indicators: China vs. major economies

Country	Total patent applications (by applicant origin 2012)[a]	R&D expenditures 2012 (% of GDP)[b]
China	18,627	1.6 %
USA	51,207	2.7 %
Germany	18,855	2.9 %

[a]World Intellectual Property Organization (http://ipstatsdb.wipo.org)
[b]OECD Science, Technology and Industry Scoreboard 2013 (http://www.oecd-ilibrary.org)

First drafted in 2009, these policies state that the government would only procure products that contain 'indigenous innovation' (innovation work leading to intellectual property held by Chinese companies). The original draft stated these products would have "locally owned" intellectual property and have a Chinese brand-name, but in 2010, a revised draft notice reduced the stringent IPR requirements. Still, the message is clear: the Chinese government strongly supports domestic innovators by offering subsidies and setting regulatory frameworks which foster indigenous innovation. This may negatively impact future business with foreign companies, but China's attempts to enhance innovation may also have positive effects: since innovation and IP protection are generally connected, the leadership will be forced to strengthen its IPR protection policies to stave off competition from lower-cost Asian countries.

INSIGHT: Dr. Stephen Dyer, A.T. Kearney

1) Unique attributes of China's innovation environment

Strong government support for "indigenous" innovation

Expanding innovation and higher value-added industries is a main pillars of the Chinese government's long term strategy. The government fosters indigenous innovation and many explicit or implicit government policies make technology transfer or sharing with local Chinese partners a market entry requirement for western companies.

Dynamic environment with limited legal and regulatory clarity

China's legal and regulatory environment has not always kept pace with its rapid economic growth in past decades. There are still major gaps in clarity and enforcement of frequently shifting policies. Intellectual property protection remains heavily influenced by local politics.

Intelligent but inexperienced talent pool

There is a large pool of highly educated, intelligent, and energetic technical and management personnel in China. However, there have not yet been many successive generations of managers and engineers trained by professional mentors. Therefore, there is a severe shortage of experienced white collar labor. The average age and professional experience of technical and management personnel in China is about 10 years younger than those in similar positions in mature markets. For example, one client I encountered joined a major Chinese automaker after graduating from university and only three years later was appointed to be program manager of the company's most important car development program, something unthinkable in a mature market.

Hierarchical but community and team-based culture

China has a strong "top-down" hierarchical management culture, which often stifles independent thinking so critical for innovation. Innovation is also suppressed by the silo mentality pervasive in many Chinese organizations and discomfort with working across functions in a matrix structure (chap. 30). That said, China is also a "community - based" culture in which individuals derive fulfillment from putting community and family interests above personal interests – this makes team spirit strong.

2) Implications for western companies innovating in China

Showcase your China-based innovation efforts for the Chinese government

- Build the perception that you foster local innovation to open doors and facilitate obtaining permission for business operation and expansion – e.g., foreign automakers agree to jointly develop products, including electric vehicles, and build JV brands with their Chinese joint venture partners to obtain approval for expanding production capacity – often form is more important than substance in these cases.

Thoughtfully define and communicate the role of your China-based innovation and product development team

- Clarify and communicate what you wish to innovate in China, and why, to guide your overall approach to building capacity and defining work scope.
- Carefully consider when you should evolve your China-based innovation and product development along the spectrum of possible roles, including:
    - Supporting the manufacture of foreign-designed products in China
    - Adapting existing products for China
    - Developing new products for China
    - Developing new products in China for the world
- Fully take advantage of local Chinese staff who truly understand local market needs to not only innovate for China, but also for other emerging markets.

Establish systems and culture for rapidly creating, sharing, and using knowledge

- Provide formal training and rigorously apply systematic problem solving (e.g., using PDCA), concise and logical communication (e.g., using A3 reports), and fact-based decision making.
- Establish processes to systematically gather best practices and lessons learned, and strictly require teams to create and consult them.

- Provide incentives to take risks and allow for failure on less critical activities to build visceral first-hand experience within your young innovation team.

Adapt HR policies to the China environment

- Pay above market-average compensation for engineers in core technology areas to retain key talent
- Provide extensive training and exposure to new technologies and work philosophies to attract and retain talent
- Adapt more incremental job titles and job descriptions for your technical staff to allow for frequent "promotions" to satisfy the heavy importance of "status" in China

Establish strong program directors to take ownership for product creation activities throughout the product lifecycle

- Give authority and responsibility to "heavyweight" program managers to break through silos and provide cradle-to-grave responsibility for innovating and realizing increasingly high quality products that meet customer needs
- Insist on appointing such managers even though your China team may claim that no one has the requisite combination of technical and management experience. Developing this capability early on will provide a competitive advantage in China (E.g., one Chinese commercial vehicle manufacturer client of mine appointed a team of young program managers even in the face of doubts about their experience. These new leaders quickly learned and successfully brought results)

Adopt internal competition to drive innovation

- Establish multiple competing internal teams to innovate toward the same objective. However, apply this approach only for relatively investment-light innovation, not in industries that require scale and deep long-term learning, such as automotive (two major Chinese automakers both adopted internal competition across their overlapping product lines and brands to disastrous effect before backtracking and consolidating product development efforts).

The Rising Middle Class

7

Three decades of economic growth have successfully produced a large, previously non-existent middle class. Seen as crucial to political and economic stability, strengthening the middle class is now a primary focus on the government's agenda.

The leadership is well aware that it can only succeed by avoiding conflict with its continuously growing middle class. Traditionally, university students and intellectuals were considered middle class. The government kept a close eye on them, as they have often led and organized social demonstrations in China (Gifford 2008). The new middle class is different as it has built its wealth largely on the manufacturing boom. Accordingly, the state has done its best to ensure that the group is prospering, even at the expense of disgruntled peasants and workers (Elfick 2011). The leadership is actively encouraging growing consumption, spending, and loyalty to the CCP.

The designation of middle class is highly sought after in today's population. Men wear their nails long and clean to show they don't have to do manual labor. Citizens buy expensive cars and seek electronic products and brand name clothes as proof of status to demonstrate their wealth.

McKinsey & Company research (which qualifies middle class by annual disposable income 60–229 kRMB) has revealed that the geographic spread of the middle class has changed dramatically, showing that a decade ago half of the Chinese middle class lived in Tier 1 cities, whereas today, less than a quarter of the middle class are living there. However, the middle class is not diminishing in the Tier 1 cities. It is just growing at an even faster pace in smaller cities.[1] This is a trend which is likely to continue in the years to come as the middle class spreads throughout the country.

China's leaders have made their intentions clear: they will continue their efforts to move more citizens into the middle class bracket while also helping to grow the

[1] McKinsey&Company: China's next Chapter. D. Barton, Y. Chen, A. Jin: Mapping China's Middle Class, 2013, can be found at: www.mckinsey.com

© Springer International Publishing Switzerland 2015

H.R. Randau, O. Medinskaya, *China Business 2.0*, Management for Professionals,
DOI 10.1007/978-3-319-07677-5_7

wealth of the current middle class. The future growth of the middle class and its increasing diversity will give businesses multiple future opportunities. If China is successful in rebalancing the economy the new middle class could become the engine of consumer spending (Figs. 7.1 and 7.2).

TIPS, OPPORTUNITIES and WARNINGS

Warning: Framing the middle class is difficult

The term "middle class" is used frequently and China's middle class is growing in size and diversity, but geographic disparities in spending power make attempts to precisely determine financial brackets difficult. Institutes, researchers, and government agencies frequently use different dimensions to define classes. This often limits the compatibility of market data. Be advised to check carefully what other dimensions in addition to income, such as age, occupation, education and ethnic, have been used to categorize social classes.

	Annual income in kCNY	Who they are?	What are their needs?
Upper	Above 500	Private business owner/ property speculator/ Stock Market gurus / high salaried executives	• Want to show off prestige and status • Strong preference for premium brands
Upper-Middle	200 - 300	Middle management Small business owner Professionals & senior civil servant	• Care more about the recognition of their peers, and don't want be different from other • Follow popular brands • Advanced features also offer a strong appeal
Middle	100 - 150	White collar/ Common staff Junior civil servant	• Good balance of price and features • Care about value for money
Lower Middle	Below 80	New graduates Retirees Individual business owners	• Rigid and limited budget • Low cost driven • For young people trendy and novel design is also important

→ China's middle class will become the third largest in the world by 2020

Fig. 7.1 Spending habits according to class (used with kind permission from McKinsey & Company)

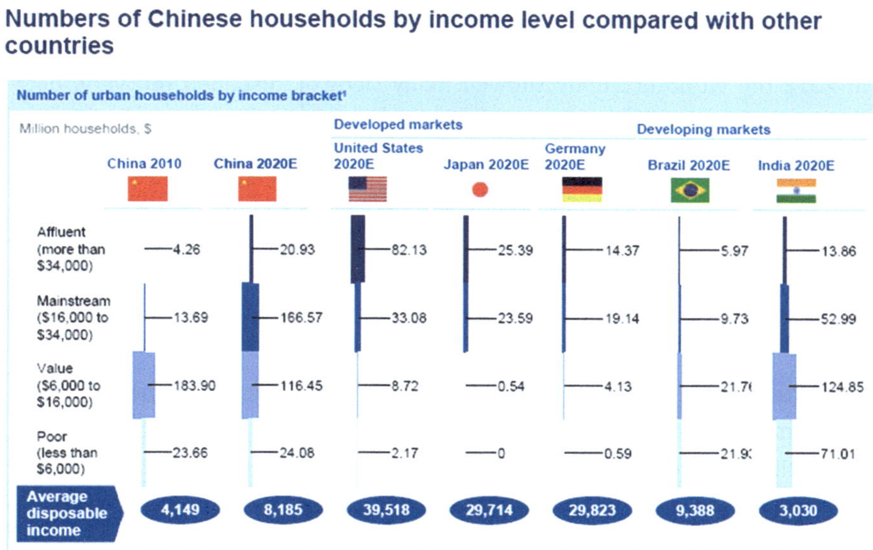

Fig. 7.2 Numbers of Chinese households by income level compared with other countries. *Source*: McKinsey Insights China—macroeconomic model update (March 2011); Canback Dangel for United States, Japan, Germany (used with kind permission from McKinsey & Company)

INSIGHT: Dr. Daniel Zisper, McKinsey & Company

In 2012 the world economy showed many signs of sustained recovery, but growth overall was still weak. China was a robust exception, as the national economy continued to evolve rapidly. In the past 12 months the number of affluent households increased by 1.8 million, Chinese consumers bought nearly 15 million passenger cars and on-line retail sales grew by 65 percent to USD 210 billion. China also began construction on 200 new skyscrapers—when they are completed, China will have surpassed the United States as the country with the most buildings taller than 152 meters.

Over the past two decades, China's strong GDP growth has been powered by government and corporate investments, primarily from state-owned enterprises. Returns have been relatively high returns and were retained or reinvested. Now a new chapter is opening in China's development, in which private consumption will begin to replace investment as the major driver of GDP growth and eventually constitute the largest share of GDP.

With rapid GDP growth has come urbanization. By 2012 over half of China's population was living in cities and the Xi administration is seeking to raise this proportion to 60 percent. Large-scale migration to the southern coastal cities, home to China's export-oriented industries, had burgeoned over the past two decades. Now this migration is expected to decline, as rural workers in inland provinces seek to work in cities closer to their hometowns. Urbanized households will continue to drive growth in average income, which is predicted to rise 46 percent over the 2013-20 period, more than three times the expected rise for rural households.

According to McKinsey analysis, by 2020 over 800 million Chinese will live in cities. China will have over 170 cities with more than 1 million inhabitants. The top 225 Chinese cities will account for around one-quarter of total global growth through 2020, and Shanghai and Beijing will have as many high-consuming middle-class residents as New York and Los Angeles.

As living standards in China continue to advance, its vast consumer market is undergoing fundamental change. Most significant is the increasing manifestation of behavior and spending patterns typical of more affluent nations. McKinsey's study of Chinese consumers has since 2005 included annual surveys that have extracted a trove of information from in-depth interviews with thousands of respondents. In 2012 the survey sample was

10,000 people aged 18 to 65, from 44 cities. Our work on these surveys has enabled us to identify key trends that will dominate the next wave of growth in the nation's consumer-goods market.

We have found that China's consumers have become increasingly sophisticated over time. While the great majority still exhibit traditional shopping patterns, carefully searching for the best deals and spending much time comparing products, new spending behaviors and patterns that resemble those found in the world's leading developed economies are rapidly appearing in China. Chinese purchasers, that is, are increasingly allowing their personal preferences to influence their purchases.

Key Chinese Consumer Trends

Pragmatism. The buoyant mood of Chinese consumers has not curtailed their tradition of saving money. On average, respondents to our 2012 survey save 22 percent of their monthly household income—eight percentage points more than their American and British counterparts saved in 2011. At the same time, China's consumers are willing to spend more for some goods and services. In 2012, for example, 46 percent of those surveyed were willing to pay a premium to achieve food safety, a further increase from the 2011 survey and a level about 30 percentage points higher than that of American and British consumers.

Trading up. Chinese consumers are increasingly trading up—buying more expensive products and services, especially in the category of leisure and entertainment. The phenomenon of trading up has been observed in many product categories, and the reasons for this rise in spending vary accordingly. Variation can also be measured by city tiers—the groupings of Chinese cities based on size (as measured by GDP and population).

Emotional but mindful of product safety. A product's "emotional" benefits are becoming increasingly important to consumers. Forty-one percent of respondents said that they would buy appliances or digital products because they enjoy them— a higher percentage than among UK shoppers (but lower than U.S. levels). At the same time, Chinese consumers are increasingly looking for reliable products, as large percentages named "a reliable brand" as one of the top five buying factors.

Brand loyalty. Despite their well-known affinity for brand-name products, Chinese consumers have shown far less brand loyalty than their Western counterparts. There is some indication that this is changing, however. In choosing among brands, 30 percent of 2012 respondents said they always buy the brands they prefer, up from 22 percent in 2009.

All about social media. Chinese consumers spend 46 minutes per day on social media, 24 percent more time than the average for U.S. consumers and 300 percent more than Koreans. Two-thirds of Chinese respondents rely on recommendations from social media sites. Many said they use social media as a primary source for learning about new products.

A "new mainstream"

Changes to consumers' economic status continue to be the most important factor in shaping the consumer landscape. Chinese consumers are certainly getting richer fast: the disposable income of urban consumer households is expected to double between 2010 and 2020, from about USD 4,000 to about USD 8,000. At that level, Chinese consumers will approach the buying power of South Korea's but still significantly trail levels seen in leading developed countries, such as the United States (USD 35,000) and Japan (about USD 26,000).

A dichotomy is emerging in China, more rapidly than expected, between a "new mainstream" middle class, on the one hand, and "mass" households on the other. Mass households, those that are still in the early stages of income growth and are still seeking to satisfy needs for basic goods and services, comprise 71 percent of the total. These households have an annual disposable income of between RMB 37k and 106k.

The new mainstream is growing, however. Our projections suggest that this segment will comprise half of all households by 2020. New mainstream consumers are experienced buyers, and are reshaping Chinese consumer habits and setting trends as they grow their way toward 2020. Nearly half of new mainstream consumers are between 18 and 34 years old; three-quarters live in tier 1 and 2 cities and an even higher percentage live in coastal clusters. The profile of these new mainstream consumers resembles that of middle-class consumers in leading developed countries. They are more willing to trade up and shop on emotion, be brand-loyal and use the Internet channel.

Implications

For China and the world economy, the implications of Chinese consumer spending growth are enormous. High- and middle-income households with stronger purchasing power are expanding everywhere in China. Chinese consumers are becoming more numerous and more diversified and sophisticated in their shopping patterns, a shift that demands of companies differentiated brand and product portfolios, pricing, and marketing strategies. Brands need to be tailored to the specific needs of different consumer segments. Strong corporate brands will need to build national presence and attain recognition among consumers, retailers, and the government, while portfolios of regional brands will have to be designed to address local tastes. Companies need to provide a full spectrum of prices to drive trial and conversion in inner China and in lower-tier cities, while encouraging consumers in coastal clusters and higher-tier cities to "trade up."

Marketing strategies need to encompass multiple touch-points, including television, in-store, and new media. The on-line channel is becoming more important in China, and to take advantage of the trend, companies will have to invest in the online consumer experience. Social media is an especially important factor in China, where the new mainstream consumer population is disproportionately young. Nevertheless, in the short term, the in-store experience is still of paramount importance, and companies that aspire to excellence at the point of sales will position themselves for success.

Suggestions for Further Reading

Forbes	www.forbes.com
Gifford, R. (2008). *China Road: a journey into the future of a rising power*. New York: Random House Trade Paperback.	
McKinsey & Company	www.mckinsey.com
The Hurun Research Institute	www.hurun.net

References

Elfick, J. (2011). Class formation and consumption among middle-class professionals in Shenzhen. *Journal of Current Chinese Affairs, 40*(1), 187–211.

Gifford, R. (2008). *China road: a journey into the future of a rising power*. New York: Random House Trade Paperback.

8 The Banking Sector

Along with structural changes in the economy, China's financial sector has also opened during the past decades. Until the early 1980s, China's only financial institution was China's central bank, the People's Bank of China (PBC). Under the government's central planning, the PBC was responsible for both currency policymaking and credit operation. The period from 1982 until 2003, saw significant changes in Chinese banking. The omnibus responsibilities of the PBC were pruned and the banking sector split into public and private industries.

In the 1980s, the four major commercial divisions of the PBC were divided into individual businesses: The industrial and commercial division, the foreign currency division, the agricultural division, and the infrastructure division. Each division was transformed into a separate commercial bank. Since then, they have adopted the moniker of the "Big Four". Later, they were carved out of the PBC with the objective of eventually being run like private banks.

China entered another stage of reform in 2003, when regulatory powers were officially segregated and supervisory authority was given to various agencies. The PBC, as China's central bank, now only concentrates on the formulation of monetary policies, such as setting the interest rates for loans and deposits, the level of reserve requirements, and other ratios affecting bank liquidity. All other responsibilities have been transferred to three specialist commissions authorized to regulate the banking, securities, and insurance sectors. Attempts to further privatize banks and reduce government interference in loan decisions were stopped in 2005 (Walter and Howie 2011).

At present, the Chinese banking system is highly complex: Over 4,000 banks operate in the finance sector, with over 200,000 business outlets.[1] However, the *Big Four* state-owned commercial banks, along with the Bank of Communication (BoComm) hold the most significance: they dominate the sector in assets and hold the majority of government bonds and household deposits.

[1] China Banking Regulatory Commission Annual Report 2010.

© Springer International Publishing Switzerland 2015
H.R. Randau, O. Medinskaya, *China Business 2.0*, Management for Professionals,
DOI 10.1007/978-3-319-07677-5_8

The *Big Four*, called the Industrial and Commercial Bank of China (ICBC), the China Construction Bank, the Bank of China (BOC) and the Agricultural Bank of China, are true giants today. ICBC and ABC have over 400,000 employees and all four of them are ranked within the top 10 of the world's biggest banks by Tier-1 capital. Each of the Big Four banks entered the stock market (listed in Hong Kong and Shanghai) with historically large IPOs. But even though big-name foreign banking institutions have invested in these restructured banks, they remain majority state-controlled. Without a doubt they are connected to the state treasury, which is clearly displayed by the fact that key personnel used to work in regulatory agencies and vice versa.

They *Big Four* also enjoy huge profits, as regulations protect them from competition. For example, their profits equaled 3 % of China's GDP in 2012. In theory the *Big Four* have freedom to lend to any sectors at will, but in practice their business concentrates in traditional sectors and on the support of State-Owned-Enterprises (SOEs).

Apart from the Big Four, three policy banks (State Development Bank of China (SDBC), Agricultural Development Bank of China (ADBC) and Export Import Bank of China (EIBC)) play an important role in the finance sector. Established in 1995 to relieve the *Big Four* of their state-directed lending role, these banks are responsible for financing economic development, trade, and state-invested projects.

The largest non-state-owned banks are joint-stock commercial banks (JSCB) such as the China Merchants Bank, the China CITIC Bank, and China Minsheng. The equity ownership of this group is typically distributed among the state and private investors. Even though they are permitted to engage in various banking services, they loan more to the private sector and small to medium enterprises.

At the next level are more than 140[2] city commercial banks which have evolved from urban credit co-operatives. Due to their history, they operate mainly in the city of their headquarters. Lately these banks have been diversifying their shareholder base and merging and extending their business outside their home regions.

On the lowest tier are over 2,000 collectively owned credit co-operatives which provide credit to small and medium-sized enterprises and individuals. Foreign funded commercial banks account for only about 2 % of assets in the Chinese banking industry. Close to 200 foreign banks were operating in China in 2012,[3] yet their role has continued to be constrained by China's lending caps and slow approvals. If there is a real change to be anticipated in the banking sector, it could come from other parties. For example, Internet companies are entering the financial services market and might intensify the competition in the consumer segment.

[2] China Banking Regulatory Commission Annual Report 2010.

[3] Foreign banks in China 2012, can be found at: www.pwc.com

TIPS, OPPORTUNITIES and WARNINGS

Warning: High risk of non-performing loans (NPLs)

The continued presence of state-directed lending in the financial sector, especially during the 2009 economic stimulus package, has increased the risk of non-performing loans (NPLs). The biggest risk lies in local government loans, which have been channeled into public work projects. Rating firms have expressed their concerns about the quality of these loans, as well as the weak government control exercised through the Central Bank (PBC). Thus, analyzing the risk of NPLs is important in understanding the risks embedded in the economy.

Reference

Walter, C. E., & Howie, F. J. T. (2011). *Red capitalism: the fragile financial foundation of China's extraordinary rise*. Singapore: Wiley.

9 A Regulatory Challenge: The Chinese Stock Market

Mainland China has the second-largest stock market in the world when the volumes and market capitalizations of the Shanghai (SSE) and Shenzhen (SZSE) Stock Exchanges are combined.

Opened in 1990, the stock markets have been often divided and fragmented. The government had three initial goals for the stock market:

- To put an end to free private markets, a source of social unrest,
- To fund majority state-owned enterprises, and
- To encourage the restructuring of state firms by gaining know-how from foreign investors (Walter and Howie 2001).

To prevent foreign institutions from taking control of Chinese companies, *State-*Owned Enterprise (SOE) subsidiaries only sold minority shares. Although China's stock markets developed an impressive infrastructure and continue to gain billions of capital dollars from international markets, in terms of market capitalization it is still dominated by SOEs.[1] The vast majority of the companies listed on the Chinese stock exchanges are state-owned, have state-owned parent companies that are not listed, or are hybrids of public and private enterprises in which the government floats minority interests to raise money while retaining the bulk of shares.

Today the two mainland stock exchanges are themselves state-owned and still not entirely open to foreign investors (Table 9.1).

[1] OECD Working Group on Privatization and Corporate Governance of State Owned Assets.

© Springer International Publishing Switzerland 2015

H.R. Randau, O. Medinskaya, *China Business 2.0*, Management for Professionals,
DOI 10.1007/978-3-319-07677-5_9

Table 9.1 Comparison of China's stock exchanges (2012) [World Federation of Exchanges (WFE)]

	Shanghai	Shenzhen	Hong Kong
Founded	1990	1990	1891
Market capitalization	2.6 trillion US$	1.2 trillion US$	2.8 trillion US$
World rank	7th	13th	6th
No. of companies	954	1,537	1,572
Indexes	SSE Composite Index and CSI 300	SZE Component Index	Hang Seng Index

Source: Bloomberg

9.1 Share Classification

Shares in publicly listed companies (PLCs) are classified as state-held shares, legal-person shares, or tradable shares. All shares carry the same voting and cash flow rights.

Tradable shares are divided into A-shares (Yuan-denominated, available to domestic and select qualified foreign investors), B-shares (USD-denominated, available to domestic and foreign investors), and H-shares (traded in foreign markets).

State shares are normally held by government agencies. Legal-person shares are those owned by SOEs, collectively owned enterprises, township, and village enterprises. Neither state nor legal-person shares are publicly tradable but can be transferred to domestic institutions subject to approval.

Though they are both traded on the SSE and the SZSE, A-shares and B-shares have some key differences. One prominent difference is that B-shares often trade at a discount to A-shares, and are reported to have a lower volatility.

9.2 Reputation and Volatility

Chinese stock markets have not been good indicators of the country's economic pulse. Because of displaying high volatility and being shattered by a number of fraud and insider trading cases in past years, they are often called "casinos".

The poor supervision of microcap listed companies has made it easy for even unsophisticated fraudulent actions like giving wrong statements, booking false turnover, or showing wrong profits. In some cases, China-based companies listed on U.S. stock exchanges have gained large media coverage. Typically, these companies have entered the U.S. market through reverse mergers in which the Chinese companies merged with U.S. shell companies to overcome the rigorous Securities & Exchange Commission filing requirements for an initial public offering. These companies managed to raise billions of dollars listing their shares on

U.S. and Canadian exchanges before their investors' money was lost through plummeting share prices as news of scandals broke.

Most experts agree that China's economy won't collapse because of these accounting scandals, but they certainly have eroded (foreign) investors' appetite for Chinese stocks.

The Chinese stock markets are also known for their volatility. One of the major reasons is the fact that close to half of the shares are held by private investors, while in mature markets institutions tend to control the largest percent of shares. In contrast to other markets, where exchanges only have to deal with brokers, Chinese exchanges have to handle transactions from both brokers and individual investors. China's two major exchanges in Shanghai and Shenzhen have more than 100 million registered individual accounts (China Securities Depository and Clearing Corp. Ltd).

Trading in private rooms, where people gather to trade stocks in an atmosphere similar to that of betting offices in western countries, can be found in many Chinese cities. These small traders often try to profit from short-term price fluctuations. It is no surprise that stock prices are often driven by rumors and speculation rather than economic fundamentals (ratios).

In general, security regulation and supervision have improved in recent years. But delisting of trash companies is still slow, and the regulators are still facing tremendous challenges. Even with the state announcing harder audits, it must be assumed that general trust remains low. This situation certainly will be a big burden for the stock market also in the years to come.

Reference

Walter, C. E., & Howie, F. J. T. (2011). *Red capitalism: the fragile financial foundation of China's extraordinary rise*. Singapore: Wiley.

Internationalizing the RMB

10

China's currency goes by several names. Officially, Chinese Yuan (¥ or CNY) is the appropriate term, though "RMB" (*Renminbi*, "People's Currency") is interchangeable and the term "Quay" is used colloquially.

Right now the Yuan still remains a strictly controlled currency and China's financial system lacks the openness and transparency of developed countries. However, China has recognized its need for an international currency. The leadership has initiated a program of phases to internationalize the Yuan. The government aims to make the Yuan a medium of investment and exchange beyond its borders by 2020.

To this end, China has announced a package of reforms which focus on increasing the use of the Yuan in international trade and building off-shore Yuan trading centers (in Hong Kong and Singapore). The first steps in easing cross-border transactions have already been taken as the Yuan can now be bought, sold, borrowed, lent, swapped and hedged. Establishing the Yuan as a regional or even global key reserve currency will eventually lead to more flexible exchange rates and most likely to a future appreciation of the currency.

Even though appreciation might hurt China's international export competitiveness, it is expected that the government will continue seeking more flexible exchange rates since an international currency would lay exchange rate risks on foreign trade partners, thereby reducing China's exposure to the U.S. dollar. China's major obstacles will be the reformation of the financial system and the attainment of credibility so as to persuade non-residents to adopt the Yuan as a store of value rather than simply a currency for international transactions (Graph 10.1).

© Springer International Publishing Switzerland 2015

H.R. Randau, O. Medinskaya, *China Business 2.0*, Management for Professionals,
DOI 10.1007/978-3-319-07677-5_10

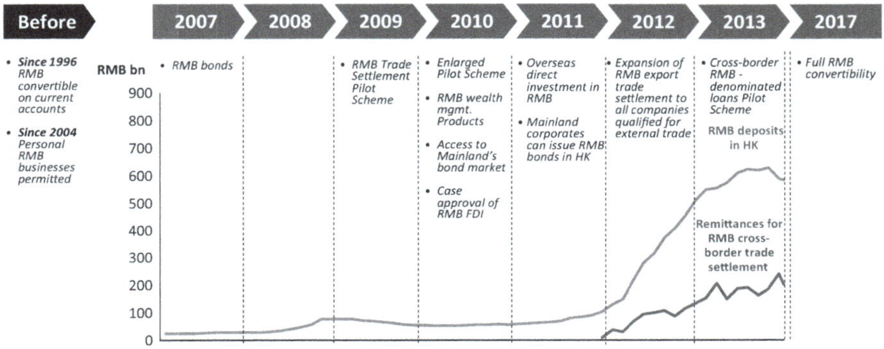

Graph 10.1 Key steps in RMB development to international currency. *Sources*: Hong Kong Monetary Authority

TIPS, OPPORTUNITIES and WARNINGS

Tip: Be aware of complicated financial cross-border transactions

The limited convertibility of the Yuan can make business with Chinese entities very time-consuming. Transactions tend to be very complex and require filling out numerous documents with various agencies. Given the potential changes in the convertibility of the Yuan, you should closely monitor announcements of any kind from the Chinese National Bank.

Warning: Increased RMB volatility risk due to the regulatory easing of trade

The regulatory easing of the RMB may compel your business partners to use it for cross-border transactions. This needs to be considered in operating your business. When the Yuan finally becomes less regulated, it also increases the volatility and your business risk.

Suggestions for Further Reading

Bloomberg	www.bloomberg.com
International Monetary Fund	www.imf.org
Hong Kong Monetary Authority	www.hkma.gov.hk
Reuters	www.reuters.com
Standard Chartered Bank	www.standardchartered.com

China's Infrastructure: An Overview 11

China's leadership recognized the importance of a well-developed infrastructure as an important driver for economic growth early. China's transportation, electricity, and communication infrastructure has improved rapidly since first given priority in the 7th FYP (1986–1990) (Fig. 11.1).

Without a doubt, the nation has made great progress in clearing its backlog of much-needed infrastructure improvements. Infrastructure investments amounted to a share of 9–11 % of GDP over the last decade. China leads the world in infrastructure investment. The stock of infrastructure investment (the value of all past investment adjusted for depreciation) is 76 % of GDP,[1] but the stock per person is still as low as approx. 10 % of that of the United States. From this perspective China is still-underinvested.

Certainly, this impressive data does not explain how much these investments have contributed to economic growth because high ratios of investment of GDP themselves do not indicate an efficient allocation. Many super-modern but costly projects were built, yet remain underused. The latest infrastructure building boom, which was mainly driven by the fiscal stimulus program China enacted in 2009 to avert the contagious effects of global economic slowdown, has even worsened the situation. Perhaps China has built too much infrastructure and is too far ahead of the economic development.

In any case, many projects completed in the past have been rendered deficient. Bumpy roads and the collapse of several bridges in recent years have indicated that the quality is far below western standards. Other worries center around the maintenance and operational costs of China's infrastructure objects, which will burden local governments with huge expenses in the future. High-speed trains are a good example of these concerns. Viewed as an expression of the nation's technological progress, the leadership had several tracks built at high costs. Consequently, ticket

[1] McKinsey & Company: Infrastructure Productivity. How to Save $1 Trillion a Year, January 2013, can be found at: www.mckinsey.com

© Springer International Publishing Switzerland 2015

H.R. Randau, O. Medinskaya, *China Business 2.0*, Management for Professionals,
DOI 10.1007/978-3-319-07677-5_11

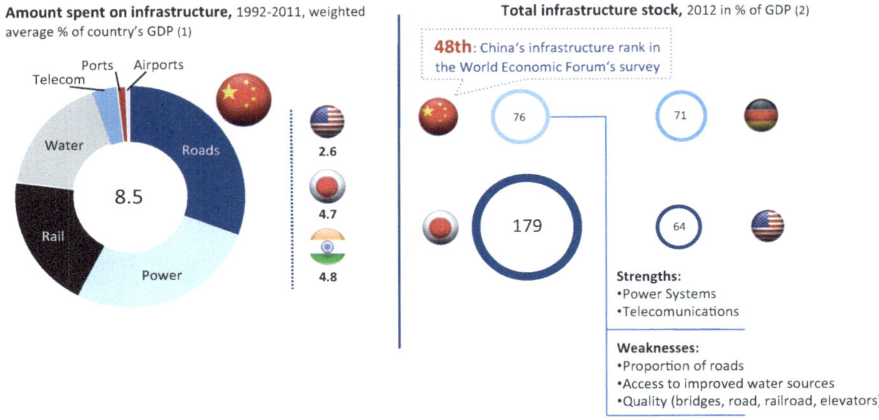

Fig. 11.1 China Infrastructure. *Sources*: (1) HIS Global Insight; GWI; IEA; ITF; McKinsey Global Institute analysis, IMF, World Bank, Ministry of Transport; (2) HIS Global Insight; Global Water Intelligence; International Transport Forum, Organization for Economic Co-operation and Development (OECD); OECD's perpetual inventory method; McKinsey Global Institute

prices are too high for average Chinese to afford and the demand is limited. In addition, these high-speed trains are difficult to operate. Two major deadly collisions revealed that China might not yet be ready for such complex systems.

Looking ahead, China's future plans continue to be ambitious. The leaders will keep investing a great deal of resources in infrastructure projects. The government may slow down the infrastructure to GDP ratio in coming years, but given the stock of investment the country will remain in good position. One of China's major objectives is to bring the entire nation's urban infrastructure up to second-world-country level. Another main goal is to narrow the development gap between the coastal areas and western parts of the country.[2]

11.1 Railways

China operates the world's longest high-speed rail network spanning about 13,000 km[3] (Japan: 2,450 km, Germany: 1,410 km) and they have an ambitious plan to have the largest, fastest, and most technologically advanced high-speed railway system in the world in the coming years. Bolstered by a ¥700 billion urban rail investment in the 12th FYP period (2011–2015), China plans to operate 25,000 km of high-speed railway by 2020.

[2] McKinsey Quarterly, *China's next chapter: Chinese infrastructure: The big picture*, Yougang Chen, Stefan Matzinger, and Jonathan Woetzel, 2013 Number 3, pp. 8–15.

[3] Xinhua (www.xinhua.org).

11.2 Roads and Expressways

China's first expressway was built in 1988 and until 1993 there were very few others. This situation has changed dramatically. By 2012, the Expressway Network of China had a total length of 95,600 km[4] longer than the total expressway of the EU and second in the world only to the U.S. (approx. 100,000 km). If the 12th FYP succeeds, China will surpass the U.S. by 2015. A central part of these investments is the so called 7,918 network: 7 radial roads from the center of Beijing, 9 north-south lines, and 18 east-west lines.

11.3 Air Traffic

China is investing heavily on air infrastructure, with a planned 70 new passenger airports between 2012 and 2015. Currently, Chinese airplanes carry the second largest number of yearly passengers, and Beijing Capital Airport is the second busiest airport in the world.

[4] Xinhua (www.xinhua.org).

Part II

Challenges

PRC faces many challenges in the *China 2.0* era, mainly due to uncontrolled or unbalanced growth, changing demographics, and weak governance. Some of these problems are so urgent that they need to be addressed promptly, as they could otherwise even put social or political stability at risk.

This part is intended to familiarize you with the details of the key challenges. Understanding them is of utmost importance, because they need to be met by the government with reform and innovation. Whatever China decides to do about these challenges, it will have a direct impact on the nation's economic potential and structure. Only those managers who carefully evaluate the effects of these challenges will draw the right conclusion for their businesses and be in the position to respond with innovative products and business models that enable their companies to exploit the tremendous opportunities China offers at its new development stage.

12 Energy: Growth, Supplies, and Dependencies

PRC is the world's biggest overall energy consumer.[1] Once a major exporter of both oil and coal, China is increasingly relying on imports to cover its need for natural resources. The enormous appetite for energy has made power outages a regular problem—which could hamper future economic growth. The government, to some effect, has promoted reduction in energy intensity (energy consumed per unit of GDP), but absolute consumption continues to increase.

Though China is one of the biggest crude oil producers, given its population and increasing oil consumption, its resources are too limited for self-sufficiency. China has been forced to import large and increasing quantities of crude oil through relationships with oil-rich nations in the Middle East and Africa. Some of these relationships, involving countries with questionable political records, have caused global criticism.

To reduce their dependence on imports and ensure reliable supplies of gasoline, diesel, jet-fuel, and other resources, Chinese National Oil Companies (NOC's) have acquired international reserves, created joint ventures with resource holders, and encouraged oil refinery expansions.

China's electricity generation is still dominated by fossil fuels, particularly coal: not only is China the world's biggest coal consumer, but it consumes nearly half of the world's total. Here again, despite heavy domestic production, consumption exceeds production significantly, and China has become the world's second largest importer. As coal is cheaper to import from Southeast Asia and provides tremendous energy security, it will likely continue to power the country in the foreseeable future.

[1] International Energy Agency (www.iea.org). Calculated in a metric which represents all forms of energy consumed, including crude oil, nuclear power, coal, natural gas and renewable sources such as hydropower.

© Springer International Publishing Switzerland 2015

H.R. Randau, O. Medinskaya, *China Business 2.0*, Management for Professionals,
DOI 10.1007/978-3-319-07677-5_12

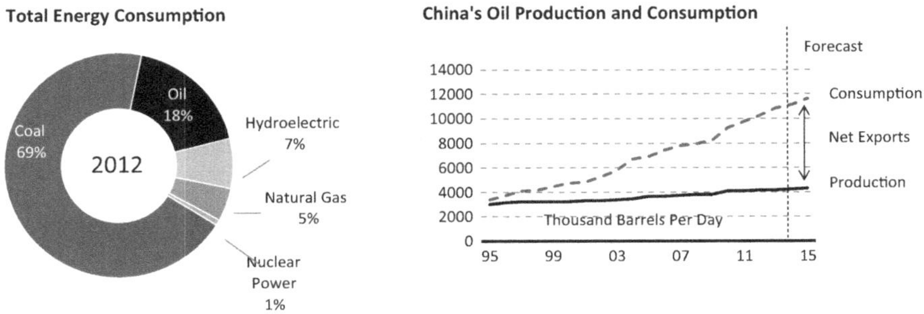

Fig. 12.1 China's energy sources. *Source*: CIA World Factbook, EIA Short-Term Energy Outlook

The Chinese government recognizes the harmful effects on the environment as well as the fact that coal is an exhaustible resource. Hence, they are implementing several measures to reduce the country's reliance on coal.

Currently providing only approx. 2 % of total energy (much lower than the global average), the Chinese government has made clear its intentions to increase nuclear power's share—multifold—by 2020. Though plans have been revised and thorough investigations were undergone after the 2012 Fukushima incident in Japan (and ensuing public apprehensions across China), China's nuclear power plans remain substantial.

The Chinese government has also given priority to the development of natural gas and renewable power sources. Natural gas consumption—a cleaner alternative to coal—has already been increasing. Already, China is the world's largest investor in renewable energy (Liu and Goldstein 2013), with renewable energy largely stemming from hydropower, such as the Three Gorges Dam (the largest hydroelectric power station on the globe). China is also the world leader in wind and solar power (Fig. 12.1).

Suggestions for Further Reading

Energy Policy	www.journals.elsevier.com
International Energy Agency	www.iea.org
The Guardian	www.theguardian.com

Reference

Liu, J., & Goldstein, D. (2013). Understanding China's renewable energy technology exports. *Energy Policy, 52*, 417–428.

13 Securing Resources: China's Diminishing Supply

Despite its size and unrivaled supply of labor, China lacks the natural resources it needs to fuel its production and growth. Generally low resource efficiency and continuing environmental issues exacerbate this shortage. As a result, many natural resources have to be imported in large amounts (Fig. 13.1).

In fact, Chinese demand has played a prominent role in driving the global commodity prices upwards and propelled a boom in resource rich regions like Australia and emerging economies in Africa and Latin America. E.g. China is the largest soy importer and its demand is so high that it would have to increase its farmland by almost 50 % to grow its own soy (Green et al. 2012). However, China is rich in rare earth metals, such as antimony, vanadium, and zinc, and exporting these has helped mitigate its resource deficit.

The Chinese government directly subsidizes seeds (e.g. grain, rice, wheat, maize and soybeans) and agricultural machinery purchases. It also strongly encourages lending to farmers. These are measures in an effort to boost agricultural production and to raise famers' incomes. It also still controls many commodities. This often leads to artificially low commodity prices and supports the export-oriented industry. But it also results in poor resource efficiency as can be easily seen when measuring for example the proportion of fossil fuels and energy consumption to GDP. As labor costs will continue to rise, China's manufacturers will be hard-pressed to maintain cost advantages and will be forced to find a less resource-intensive approach to growth (Jacques 2012). Together with the leader's goals of increasing energy and carbon efficiency to avoid further pollution it may lead to reforms in the administrative control of commodities. That could gradually bring commodity prices in line with their real market levels.

China's leaders are conscious that continued growth depends on steady, affordable access to more natural resources than the country can produce, so to ensure resource security they have established strong foreign relations with resource-rich countries. These include nations in Africa, Southeastern Asia, Australia, and the Middle East. Such countries are enticed by the opportunity to sell their resources at

© Springer International Publishing Switzerland 2015

H.R. Randau, O. Medinskaya, *China Business 2.0*, Management for Professionals,
DOI 10.1007/978-3-319-07677-5_13

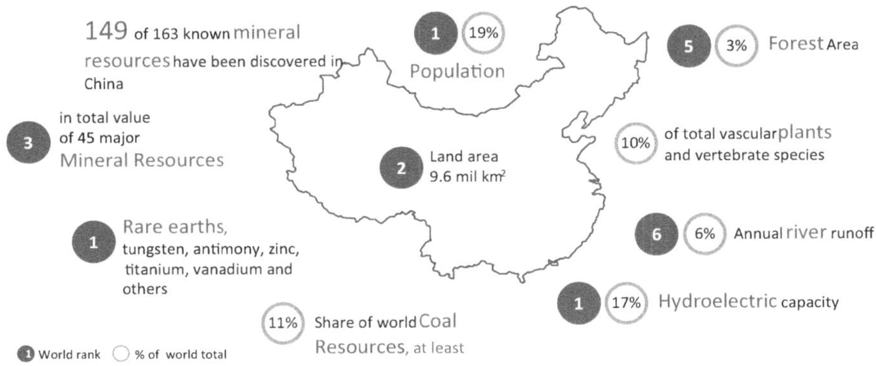

Fig. 13.1 Supply and World Rank of China's natural resources (Staiger et al. 2009; Zhao 1994)

high prices, import the goods China produces, and access Chinese markets for their own domestic goods.

However, many developed nations view China's growing power in other parts of the world with distrust, citing the PRC's foreign policy in resource-laden nations as lacking conditionality or altruism. Other worries center around the PRC's territorial claims. For example, the claim in the South China Sea directly affects neighboring countries, such as the Philippines and Vietnam. China's quest for fishing grounds raises questions about its adherence to international obligations.

Despite the cold, commercial appearance of China's relationships with many of these countries, the state government is increasingly working to improve China's reputation and soft power throughout the world. For example, China finances many infrastructure projects and scholarship programs to Chinese universities for its developing trade partners. Still, many countries are caught between fearing China's influence in their affairs, and wanting to fill China's growing economic demands (Rein 2012).

References

Green, S., Ofon, A., & Rosen, B. (2012). *China – On China's animal feed farm.* Standard Chartered Global Research.

Jacques, M. (2012). *When China rules the world: The end of the Western world and the birth of a new global order* (p. 207). London: Penguin Books.

Rein, S. (2012). *The end of cheap China: Economic and cultural trends that will disrupt the world* (Chapter 8). Hoboken: Wiley.

Staiger, B., Friedrich, S., & Schütte, H. W. (Eds.). (2009). *Das große China-Lexikon: Geschichte, Geographie, Gesellschaft, Politik, Wirtschaft, Bildung, Wissenschaft, Kultur.* Darmstadt: Wissentschaftliche Buchgesellschaft.

Zhao, S. (1994). *Geography of China: Environment, resources, population and development.* New York: Wiley.

14 Intense Growth: The Environmental Impact

China's phenomenal growth has been achieved in a largely inefficient, resource-intensive way, similar to western countries in the early and mid-twentieth century. In the past, environmental effects were a secondary consideration in the pursuit of economic growth, and the level of environmental awareness within the population and even the government has been very low.

The results are clear: today, China is the world's largest polluter, with 16 of the world's 20 most-polluted cities.[1] Acid rain affects a third of the Chinese territory[2] and there is widespread ground contamination and the overuse of fertilizer. Therefore, the PRC ranks 118th on the Environmental Performance Index (EPI).[3]

Air pollution is certainly the most prominent concern, as China is the world's biggest emitter of carbon dioxide, largely driven by its coal reliance. The air quality is appalling. Especially in urban centers, the exposure to fine particles is multiple times higher than what the World Health Organization (WHO) considers unhealthy.

Another of the nation's major concerns is water shortage. The per capita water availability is only one-quarter of the world's average[4] and water resources are distributed unevenly between a relatively wet south and a dry north. Approximately 60 % of Chinese land is classified as climate in the arid or climate in the semi-arid (Warburton and Horn 2007). Desert already covers a quarter of the country and is growing by 5,000 km^2 a year. The water shortage is largely because one-third of industrial waste water and more than 90 % of household sewage is released into rivers and lakes without being treated,[5] at present, three-quarters of river water is unsuitable either for drinking or fishing (Yusuf and Saich 2008) and approx. 90 %

[1] Blacksmith Institute (www.worstpolluted.org).

[2] Third of China Hit by Acid Rain, 27.08.2006, can be found at: http://news.bbc.co.uk

[3] Environmental Performance Index (EPI) 2014, developed by Yale and Columbia university that ranks 178 countries (www.epi.yale.edu).

[4] *Climate Change Threatening Water Supply*, 25.04.2011, can be found at: www.chinapost.com.tw

[5] Climate & Development Knowledge Network (www.cdkn.org).

© Springer International Publishing Switzerland 2015

H.R. Randau, O. Medinskaya, *China Business 2.0*, Management for Professionals,
DOI 10.1007/978-3-319-07677-5_14

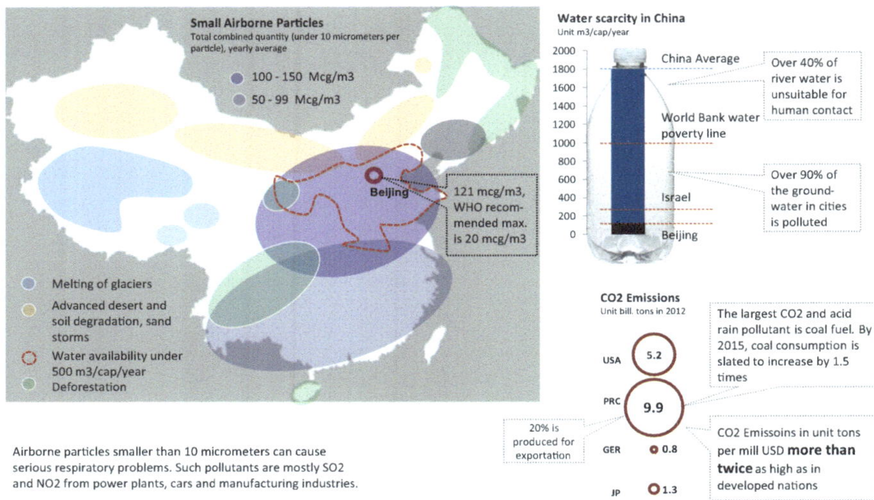

Fig. 14.1 Overview of pollution in China. *Sources*: China statistical yearbook, World bank, BP, WHO, State Environmental Protection Administration of China

of ground water is so dirty that it cannot be used for consumption, industry or agriculture.[6] Thus, 300 million people now lack access to clean drinking water (Fig. 14.1).[7]

Environmental protection will play a larger role in the China 2.0 era. The Chinese leadership has already begun to recognize the importance of preserving the environment—mainly because it is aware that further ecologic disasters may put huge constraints on economic growth. On paper China has set up some of the most advanced environment protection policies in the world, with substantial investments into carbon control, forest preservation, and energy efficiency; in practice, results have been modest. It must be expected that reinforcement will be much stronger in coming years.

TIPS, OPPORTUNITIES and WARNINGS

Opportunity: Becoming environmentally-conscious

The need for higher energy efficiency and less pollution might be a great opportunity for businesses with innovative technologies. It must be assumed that the government will strengthen its efforts to improve efficiency and the use of regenerative power. The prominent existence of solar panels on residential houses might be just a first step of the future to come.

[6] Ministry of Environmental Protection (http://english.mep.gov.cn).

[7] WWF China (http://en.wwfchina.org).

References

Warburton, J., & Horn, L. (2007). China's environmental crisis: What does it mean for development? *Development, 3*, 48–56.

Yusuf, S., & Saich, T. (2008). *China urbanizes: Consequences, strategies, and policies*. Washington, DC: The World Bank.

Demographic Dilemmas 15

China's demographics have been largely influenced by the One-child Policy which slowed China's population boom but also caused a gender imbalance through selective abortions. Today, China is facing the problems of an aging society, as life expectancy increases and birth-rates decrease. This will change the dynamics of China's workforce and may challenge the competitiveness of their future economy.

15.1 One-Child Policy

Mandated nationwide in 1979, the One-Child Policy restricts Chinese parents to a single child, with limited exceptions. Couples who violate the regulation have to pay high fines and face the fact that their children will not be able to attend school unless the parents pay for it out of their own pocket.

Though criticized for its social implications, the policy successfully slowed down population growth. The One-Child principle has become understood as a necessary measure in Chinese society.

As the percentage of elderly Chinese citizens is growing rapidly, the leadership has begun to relax the policy. The latest adjustments allow urban couples to have two children as long as one parent is an only child. Ethnic minorities and rural couples are permitted to have two offspring if their first child is a girl.

Interestingly, an increasing number of urban couples are happy with only one child, since it leaves them enough funds for a good education and a higher disposable income for better housing and health care.

15.2 Gender Imbalance

The one-child-policy together with the primacy many couples still place on having a son, has led to frequent sex-selective abortions. Though checking the gender before birth is strongly forbidden, the male-female ratio at birth is one of the highest

© Springer International Publishing Switzerland 2015
H.R. Randau, O. Medinskaya, *China Business 2.0*, Management for Professionals,
DOI 10.1007/978-3-319-07677-5_15

in the world. This gender balance is slated to continue and by 2020, men below of the age 20 are expected to outnumber women by 40 million.[1] Interestingly, wealthy families tend to welcome female and male babies equally.

15.3 Aging Society

China is a rapidly aging society, and as life expectancy rises (currently 73.5 years) an increasing proportion of Chinese will be over 60. If the One-child Policy continues, the portion of the population over 65 is expected to rise from 10 to about 15 % by 2020 (Riley 2004). Though these numbers remain low compared to other developed countries like Germany (31 %) and Japan (34 %) they still impose a heavy economic burden on younger working people.

This shift will put strong pressure on both the country's social security system and its economic growth. Expenditures for age-related programs are expected to increase sharply, with exploding healthcare costs and pension problems. The graying population may also suffer labor-shortages and increasing personal costs, eventually weakening China's global competitiveness.

Populations are expected to reach crisis level by 2035 when every pensioner is supported by less than two Chinese taxpayers.

15.4 Workforce

China has the largest workforce in the world, 34 % (2012) of which is employed in the agricultural sector.[2] Since most developed countries have less than 10 % of their workforce in agriculture, continued transition towards industrial jobs is likely—driving urbanization, and creating new social challenges for the government as productivity and incomes increase. Growing human resources costs have driven manufacturers to produce in more central and western provinces in China, while developed coastal provinces have begun accumulating more complex, technological production jobs. China's workforce on the whole is moving up the technological ladder, changing labor demographics and driving human capital costs. But the country's supply of cheap labor is far from exhausted.

Women play an important role in the workforce. Their participation is high compared to other countries,[3] helped by the one-child policy which has freed women from caring for large families, and favorable labor laws (Graphs 15.1 and 15.2).

[1] *Gendercide: the Worldwide War on Baby Girls*, 04.03.2010, can be found at: www.economist.com

[2] China Statistical Yearbook (www.stats.gov.cn/tjsj/ndsj/2013/indexeh.htm).

[3] *Women and Work: Closing the Gap*, 26.11.2011, can be found at: www.economist.com

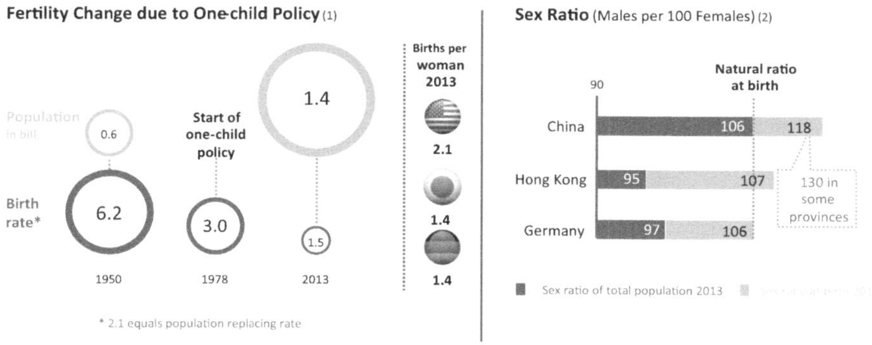

Graph 15.1 China's changing demographics. *Sources*: (1) China Statistics Yearbook, Japan Statistical Yearbook, World Bank Database, U.S. Census Bureau; (2) CIA, Shanghai Daily

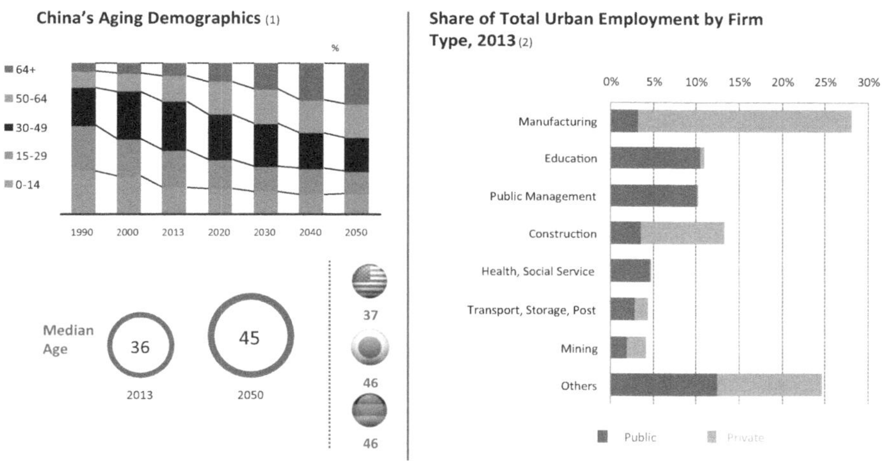

Graph 15.2 China's aging society and workforce. *Sources*: (1) CIA World Factbook, World Population Prospects United Nations, China Statistical Yearbook, Worldbank; (2) China Statistical Yearbook

Reference

Riley, N. E. (2004). China's population: New trends and challenges. *Population Bulletin: A Publication of the Population Reference Bureau, 59*, 3–36.

16 Social Concerns

Several prominent social issues strike at the heart of Chinese society and may threaten its very structure. As in many developing nations, concerns are dominated by monetary considerations and center around personal well-being, financial stability and base social coverage. Concerns also include a lack of judicial fairness, widespread bribery (Chap. 21), heavy censorship (Chap. 23), and limited freedom of speech. A 2013 survey[1] ordered the biggest social concerns amongst the Chinese public as follows (Table 16.1).

A deeper understanding of these concerns can be attained by examining the types of stories that continue to gain wide coverage in the media. If they are government related they are usually covered up or severely censored, but those that do become public often gain significant notoriety. A few recent well-known stories are listed below.

16.1 Abuse of Power and Status

China's central authoritarian structure often gives government officers unchecked opportunities to abuse their power. Despite the central government's declared opposition to corruption (Chap. 21), many officials have been involved in scandals:

Shanghai Pension Scandal In 2006, it was revealed that Shanghai party chief Chen Liangyu and other high ranking officials used social security funds as their personal piggy bank, diverting about a third of all Shanghai's social security funds into real estate and road investment projects.

[1] PEW Research Center (http://ww.pewresearch.com), *Public Concerns in China Survey 2013*.

© Springer International Publishing Switzerland 2015

H.R. Randau, O. Medinskaya, *China Business 2.0*, Management for Professionals,
DOI 10.1007/978-3-319-07677-5_16

Table 16.1 Top 10 social concerns

1. Rising prices	2. Corrupt officials
3. Income and wealth gap	4. Air pollution
5. Water pollution	6. Food safety
7. Quality of manufactured goods	8. Old age insurance
9. Safety of medicine	10. Corrupt business people

Source: PEW Research Center 2013 Public Concerns in China Survey

The Bo Family Scandal In 2012, prominent party member and Chongqing governor Bo Xilai was expelled from the party and faced charges for abuse of power, bribe taking, and numerous illicit relationships. His wife, Gu Kailai, was convicted in the murder of British businessman Neil Heywood and Bo is alleged to have been involved.

Li Gang Incident In 2010, Li Qiming, son of local vice-president of police Li Gang, hit two students while drunk driving, killing one and fracturing the other's leg. He then continued driving in attempt to drop his girlfriend at her dorm. But when stopped by police he shouted "Go ahead, sue me if you dare. My dad is Li Gang!" As uproar spread on the Internet about the incident, the government made an extensive attempt to suppress it, infuriating the public. Eventually, Li Qiming was imprisoned.

16.2 Egoistic Culture

Decades of poverty instigated by the unsuccessful "Great Leap Forward" and the Cultural Revolution have contributed to a sometimes egoistic culture. Often, Chinese will seek the good of themselves and their family before anything else. While this has led to a strong drive for success, and may even have contributed to China's strong economic advances, this mindset has societal costs.

Death of Wang Yue In October 2011, 2 year old Wang Yue was run over first by a van, and then her legs were run over by a large truck. In the meantime, at least 18 people walked by. Neither vehicle stopped, and no one came to her assistance (though some stopped and stared). She was eventually helped by a female rubbish scavenger, but died of her injuries 8 days later.

Over the past several years, there have been numerous incidents where a person was brought to safety by a helper in good faith, but still sustained injuries. For reasons often involving the inability to pay hospitable fees, the injured person has sued the helper, usually with little evidence, for being the "cause" of their injuries. The government has frequently ruled in favor of the injured person.

In light of these incidents, some officials are advocating "Good Samaritan" laws which would penalize people who refuse help those in trouble and vindicate people whose efforts are in vain.

16.3 Food Concerns

Food safety scandals have had a significant impact in China. The industry often turns a blind eye to both animal and human safety. Common issues include the overuse of chemicals in animal feed (i.e. Clenbuterol) and crop spray, protein adulteration in various foods (including the aforementioned melamine scandal), and fakery (i.e. blatantly passing off one product as another). Often, a food is made to appear, or smell, a certain way or meet a certain quota (i.e. protein, sodium quantity) at the expense of any health concerns. Perhaps the most worrying problem is that since manufacturers go to great extents to hide illegal or scandalous chemical use from inspectors, the extent of food adulteration is unknown.

Recent food scandals have included excess levels of antibiotics in chicken meat supplied to fast food chains, as well as donkey meat being recalled by large retailers due to tests showing that the product contained the DNA of other animals. Other scandals have included recycled "gutter oil" used for cooking or selling of decayed milk. In **the Melamine-Milk Scandal**, 22 companies were discovered to have used melamine in milks and infant formulas in efforts to increase their protein content. Melamine is a product used in some plastics that must be mixed with formaldehyde to dissolve in milk. As a result, 6 infants died from kidney stones and almost 52,000 were hospitalized.

16.4 Pollution

China's rapid expansion has led to many environmental concerns, with pollution one of the foremost among them. Pollution is having a substantial societal impact—affecting crops, drinking water, air freshness, and overall quality of life (Graph 16.1).

Suggestions for Further Reading

Bloomberg Business Week	www.businessweek.com
China Daily	www.chinadialy.com.cn
Chinese Academy of Social Sciences	www.bic.cass.cn
PEW Research Center	www.pewresearch.com

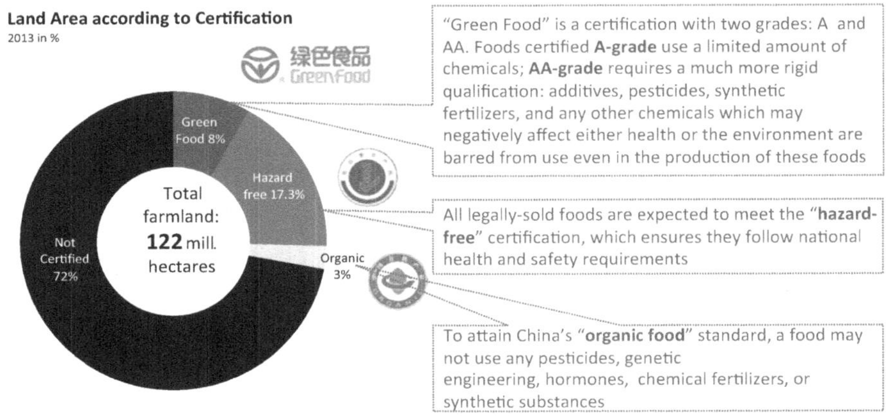

Graph 16.1 Percentage of land area according to certification. *Source*: Ministry of Agriculture of the PRC, United States International Trade Commission

High Risk: China's Real Estate 17

17.1 Land Use Rights

Ultimately, real property ownership does not exist in China. Though China's Property Law states that citizens have "the right to possess, utilize, dispose of and obtain profits from" their properties, this right is superseded by the supreme right of the state: if property ownership or transactions harm public interests or "the legitimate rights and interests of others," the state has the right to step in.

In reality, land is either owned by the state or by rural collectives for primary use in agriculture. The rural land is no longer farmed collectively even though the Constitution states that rural land is "collectively" owned. Farmers are neither allowed to sell the land they work on or the homes they live in to non-villagers nor mortgage rural property. Urban land belongs to the state and China has adopted[1] a dual tenure system under which urban land ownership is independent of land use rights. Natural persons, legal persons or organizations can acquire the right to use land for a fixed period of time. The approach is comparable to long-term ground leases (LGLs) found in western countries, with only the difference being that in western countries lessors can include entities such as corporations or private individuals whereas land in China is generally state-owned.

In both cases, the party holding land rights acquires ownership over improvements made on that property, such as new construction, for a limited period of time. However, leasing periods in the U.S. are much longer than land rights terms in China—typically between 50 and 99 years. According to the Law on Urban Land, the term of land use rights varies depending on the land use purpose. The land use rights are:

[1] Bloomberg Businessweek, Dexter Roberts: *Is Land Reform Finally Coming to China?* November 2013, can be found at: http://www.businessweek.com/articles/2013-11-20/is-land-reform-finally-coming-to-china

© Springer International Publishing Switzerland 2015
H.R. Randau, O. Medinskaya, *China Business 2.0*, Management for Professionals,
DOI 10.1007/978-3-319-07677-5_17

- 40 years for commercial use,
- 50 years for industrial use,
- 70 years for residential use.

Another distinction between Chinese land use rights and LGLs is that the Chinese government does not guarantee the protection of landlord-tenant laws when extending land use rights. Finally, parties in China are restricted from transferring or mortgaging land until they completely develop it according to the land use contract.

17.2 Economic Relevance

China relies heavily on property development for driving growth. The real estate market nurtures growth in industries like steel, construction and home appliances. Selling urban land to developers has been a major source of revenue for local governments. Driven by industrialization, urbanization, an emerging middle-class, and speculation, the real estate sector has soared over the past few years. Investment in residential housing rose from 2 % to 6 % of GDP between 2000 and 2012.

The result is a large overhang of empty properties. High-rise apartment buildings have quickly gone up in remote cities but are still deserted after failed attempts to attract residents. Continually misplaced investments in infrastructure and real estate have lead to 'ghost cities', empty districts, and shopping malls. But this has not stopped Chinese from purchasing real estate as they view housing as one of the best ways to invest money. The speculation caused a dramatic rise in housing prices, and as a consequence, the threat of a bursting real estate bubble has become a significant risk. Experts within the Chinese government warn that property prices are already strongly overvalued in some major cities.

Acknowledging this danger, the government has repeatedly attempted to cool property inflation and curb speculation. The government has limited the number of homes that each family can buy, instituted larger down payments on 1st and 2nd home mortgages, banned 3rd home purchases and cross-city investments, and implemented higher real estate transaction taxes. Since accommodation costs have become a growing concern for the poorer populace, leadership is determined to invest in much-needed "economic" housing projects. The current plans foresee the construction of 36 million units of social, affordable homes by 2015, accounting for 20 % of the total market.

Farmers have not profited from the boom, as they do not have the option of selling their land. Creating a rural property market would support further urbanization and could unlock a huge potential for additional consumer spending. The government has announced reformation plans, beginning with its typical approach of taking gradual steps. It has already launched numerous experiments in selected villages throughout the country. In these experiments farmers can trade rural land for construction development. Trials such as these will probably spread quickly throughout China.[2]

Certainly, a rural land reform will prove to be difficult for several reasons. First of all, it may be difficult to separate the land between farmers. Secondly, the government risks losing its current tight rein over the farmers. Finally, the industrial development will increasingly become more demanding as developers would potentially have to negotiate with multiple individual sellers instead of government agencies. It remains to be seen how fast the leaders are going to tackle this fundamental, if not historic, milestone in their reform agenda.

[2] The economist, A world to turn upside down, 2.11.2013, can be found at: http://www.economist.com/news/briefing/21588873-economic-issues-facing-novembers-plenum-chinese-communist-party-none-looms-larger

Urbanization: A Transforming Country 18

China is quickly transitioning from a rural country to an urban one. Since 2012 the urban population exceeded the rural population for the first time, rising from as low as 20 % in the early 1990s.

Urbanization has been crucial for China's investment-led growth model: rural workers have supported the manufacturing industry as cheap labor, generating growth, raising overall income and the overall productivity of the workforce. The current urbanization rate is still low compared to most developed nations, suggesting that tremendous growth is still ahead for many cities. Currently, China's cities absorb 20 million new people each year (approx. 1–1.5 % of the population).

Interestingly, many of these urban migrant workers are forced to retain their rural *hukou* registration (Chap. 29). They might move back to the countryside after they retire at the latest, because according to current regulations (Chap. 17) they can't sell their house and land in the countryside, they have no money to buy property in the city, and they are not entitled to the same welfare benefits as those of urban *hukou* holders.

Thus, it remains to be seen how the urbanization development continues. Some sources expect the share of urban population to rise to over 60 % which means that cities will add another 250 million to their populations by 2025.[1] Other experts stress the fact that the number of migrant workers looking for work in the cities has slowed since 2005 and predict also a slower urbanization rate, as they see only a limited potential for the more than 300 million remaining laborers in agriculture to migrate and find jobs in cities (Fang 2010).

No matter how fast urbanization continues, according to the *UN* it must be assumed that a large portion of China's urban growth will take place in suburbs of

[1] Preparing for China's Billion, McKinsey Global Institute, 2009, can be found at www.mckinsey.com

© Springer International Publishing Switzerland 2015
H.R. Randau, O. Medinskaya, *China Business 2.0*, Management for Professionals,
DOI 10.1007/978-3-319-07677-5_18

cities currently with under one million people.[2] It is also clear that the effects of the future mass migration will be significant and will give the government challenging tasks over the next decade:

- 40–50 million new urban households will need to be constructed,[3] and mass-transportation systems must be established. It remains questionable whether government-mandated housing will be able to deliver the millions of apartments that are needed or whether reforms are necessary to integrate the private sector in supplying for-rent housing
- Arable land will be lost due to city growth, resulting in tensions since cities depend on land sales
- Demand for energy, water, and natural resources will mount and the already heavy pollution will increase
- Social services like education and health care, particularly for migrants, will severely strain cities' funds
- China will face a significant shortage of workers in small to midsized cities
- Labor costs will sharply increase in urban areas which attract the talents of migrants (70 % of whom are 15–35 years old) (Fig. 18.1)

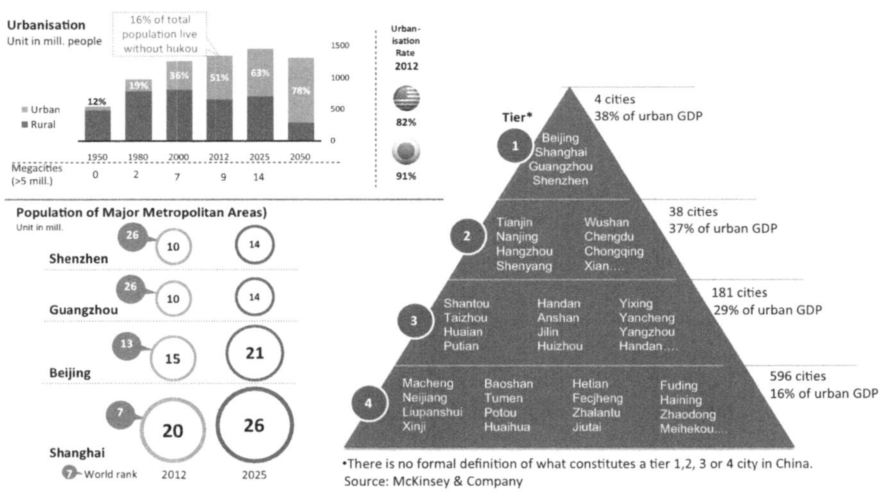

Fig. 18.1 Increasing urban populations. *Source*: China Statistical Yearbook, UN Statistic: World Population Prospects, CIA (used with kind permission from McKinsey & Company)

[2] United Nations, *World Urbanizations Prospects* (http://esa.un.org/unup/).

[3] GaveKal (http://gavekal.com).

Suggestions for Further Reading

Fang, C. (2010). Demographic transition, demographic dividend, and Lewis turning point in China. *China Economic Journal 3*(2), 107–119.	
United Nations, World Urbanizations Prospects	www.esa.un.org/unpd/wup/

Reference

Fang, C. (2010). Demographic transition, demographic dividend, and Lewis turning point in China. *China Economic Journal, 3*(2), 107–119.

19 Unequal Wealth Distribution

China's surging economy has led to a dramatic decline in poverty but has also fostered huge disparities in wealth distribution. According to World Bank, the poverty rate (people living on less than US$1.25 a day) fell from 85 % to 14 % between 1981 and 2005,[1] indicating that 600 million people climbed out of poverty. On the other hand, the income gap between rural and urban areas has widened, with the per capita disposable income in urban areas now more than 3 times as high as the rural figure. Even within cities, wealth gaps remain large.[2] A Credit Suisse report published in 2010 warned that China's wealth gap is now approaching levels until today unknown outside of Africa. The mainland is home to 251 billionaires (world rank No. 2) and 2.7 million U.S. dollar millionaires,[3] a number that is expected to expand.

Poverty remains widespread across the rural areas. Even with further economic growth it will be hard for the government to change this successfully. Currently these areas have little potential for development, and despite strong recent efforts, little growth has been realized.

Not surprisingly, China's national Gini coefficient has risen from around 0.3 in the early 1980s to exceed the warning line of 0.4 in 2000 and reached a high of 0.474 in 2012 (a coefficient of >0.5 represents an extreme income inequality with a risk of social instability and chaos) (Fig. 19.1).

---

[1] World Bank (http://data.worldbank.org).

[2] China's National Bureau of Statistics (www.stats.gov.cn/english).

[3] The Hurun Research Institute 2012 (http://www.hurun.net).

© Springer International Publishing Switzerland 2015

H.R. Randau, O. Medinskaya, *China Business 2.0*, Management for Professionals,
DOI 10.1007/978-3-319-07677-5_19

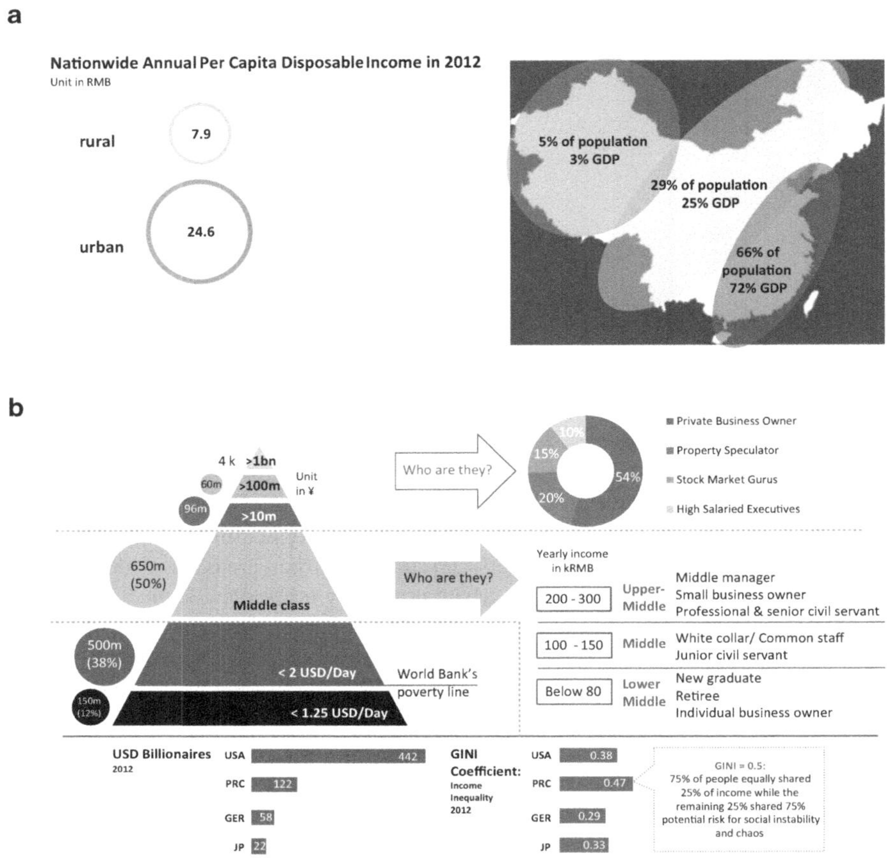

Fig. 19.1 Wealth distribution (Disposable income refers to the actual income at the dispose of members of the households which can be used for final consumption, other non-compulsory expenditure, and savings. The China Statistical Yearbook uses different definitions for the disposable income in rural and urban households. Please see http://www.stats.gov.cn/english/classificationsmethods/definitions/t20020517_402787577.htm). (**a**) *Source*: China Statistical Yearbook 2013; (**b**) Xinhua, OECD, World Bank, National Bureau of Statistic, Forbes, Hurun report, China Statistical Yearbook

China's Evolving Social Welfare System 20

China is facing big social challenges as the current pension system is unsustainable and the healthcare system has many flaws. Both systems are underfinanced, give only limited help to those in need, and require more functional and effective regulations to avoid mismanagement. The weak social welfare systems are a major reason for the high savings rate (Chap. 2) in China and are harming the government's efforts to boost spending (Chap. 5). In order to increase internal consumption, the government must find a way to boost the public's confidence and provide them with a strong sense of welfare security.

20.1 Pension

China's fledgling pension fund, which has only been in practice since the late 1980s, is financed through a mandatory deposit by employers of a portion of their employees' income. Once employees contribute payments for 15 years, they earn the legal right to receive pension paybacks. But this pension fund is already in notable debt for two main reasons:

Firstly, pension schemes suffer from evident inequality. China's pension policies follow a "double-track" system whereby government employees are subject to different rules than enterprise employees. In general, government employees receive much greater pension benefits than regular citizens. On top of this, government employees can receive their pension payments without contributing requisite funds from their gross salary.[1]

Secondly, the increasing number of senior citizens—currently over 200 million and slated to increase—is worsening funding problems. This number is being

[1] Bloomberg Businessweek, Chinese Rage at the Pension System, Dexter Roberts October 31, 2013, can be found at: http://www.businessweek.com/articles/2013-10-31/chinese-rage-at-the-pension-system

© Springer International Publishing Switzerland 2015

H.R. Randau, O. Medinskaya, *China Business 2.0*, Management for Professionals,
DOI 10.1007/978-3-319-07677-5_20

largely exacerbated by the early retirement age of only 60 for men and 50 to 55 for women.

As a consequence considerable pressure is being put on younger people—a generation already shouldering the burdens of education fees for their children, home loans, and the care of their parents. This generation will be the backbone of China's future economy, and pressing their finances too much could prove damaging China's overall growth. The system also is a burden for elderly enterprise workers. Since their pensions are generally very low, many are forced to seek jobs after official retirement. Another result is the over-allocation of human talent to government positions rather than corporate jobs: many graduates gravitate to these positions for their obvious benefits, causing further disparities in the system.

Unsurprisingly, these factors are significantly contributing to the high personal savings rate (→ INSIGHT: Chris Torrens, Control Risks). The question going forward will be whether the government will decide to extend the retirement age, continue to increase taxes (at cost for the younger generation) to sustain the country's aging society, or take any action to balance the double-track system.

20.2 Healthcare

The health of Chinese citizens has been improving significantly. Life expectancy has risen mainly due to the reduction of infectious diseases. At the same time so called "diseases of affluence", such as diabetes and cardiovascular disease, have increased rapidly.

However, healthcare remains a major topic of concern within the Chinese society for two reasons:

- Rising prices have made healthcare unaffordable for many citizens
- Millions of people still have no medical coverage, and great gaps exist between rural and urban healthcare quality and availability

With the opening of the economy, healthcare transitioned from a state-owned system to a largely market-based system. In the process, successful rural programs (for example, the "barefoot doctors") (Blumenthal and Hsaio 2005) were dismantled and alternatives were not established. In 2000, the World Health Organization rated China's health financing system as one of the most inequitable worldwide, ranking them 188th out of 191 countries, and the Chinese government has since described the health system as shameful[2] and initiated several reforms.

A current OECD report states that, given the income level in China, the proportion of doctors is rather high (Herd et al. 2010). However, average qualification levels are modest and the available beds per hospital are lower than the OECD average.

[2] Ministry of Health of the People Republic of China (http://www.moh.gov.cn), 2005.

Under the current system, hospitals are almost exclusive to urban areas while village clinics and township medical centers provide service for the rural population. Hospitals are generally owned by the state or local governments and graded according to administrative authority to which they are responsible. The higher the grade, the more skilled the staff and the better the equipment (Zhang et al. 2011).

In urban areas, one of the major flaws is that hospitals not only supply inpatient care, but are also the dominant suppliers of ambulatory care. As a consequence, hospitals treat many simple illnesses for which they are over-qualified. The hospitals are thus often fully occupied and costs tend to be high. In rural areas, the quality of service can be sub-par. Even though all medical staffs in rural facilities have had to be certified since 2002, this rule is weakly enforced and most doctors are less qualified than in urban areas.

Price regulations have posed another problem: the government, which regulates the price of the most basic health care services, has set many standard procedures below cost. To compensate for this, high-technology services like CT scans and X-ray exams which are not as regulated are often priced quite highly in an effort to deliver reasonable profit margins. To drive in extra profits, hospitals often abuse the system by over-using high-tech facilities and subscribing large quantities of high-margin pharmaceuticals (Qin 2013).

References

Blumenthal, D., & Hsaio, W. (2005). Privatization and its discontents — The evolving Chinese health care system. *The New England Journal of Medicine, 353*, 1165–1170.

Herd, R., Hu, Y. W., & Coen, V. (2010). *Improving China's healthcare system, 2010*. Paris: OECD Economics Department, OECD.

Qin, X. (2013). Too few doctors or too low wages? Labor supply of health care professionals in China. *China Economic Review, 24*, 150–164.

Zhang, X., Chen, L. W., Mueller, K., Yu, Q., Liu, J., & Lin, G. (2011). Tracking the effectiveness of health care reform in china: A case study of community health centers in a district of Beijing. *Health Policy, 100*(2–3), 181–188.

21 Corruption: Skating on Thin Ice

Corruption poses an enormous challenge to all domestic and foreign enterprises operating in China. Systematic corruption is still the rule rather than the exception, even though the government has called for tighter control. Corruption is common in the business-to-business environment and new, preventive opportunities have emerged in the public sector, such as reorganization and appraisal of state assets, the allocation of public investment funds, and the assignment and pricing of land resources. Not even public high-profile prosecutions and convictions have changed the picture. According to a Transparency International (TI) report, China is ranked 80 in 2013 (Table 21.1).

21.1 Bribery

China's anti-corruption efforts have improved since its entrance into the WTO. Currently, commercial corruption is prohibited by several laws and official bribery is prohibited by the Chinese Criminal Law. Violation of these rules leads to fines, confiscation of property, imprisonment and even the death.

Recently, China has implemented rules requiring mid-to-senior level government officials to report their investments, incomes and assets and disclose the financial details of their family members' business activities. Failing to comply with the regulations or submitting false information will lead to disciplinary measures or dismissal rather than the "informed criticism" of before. The government has also taken action to improve its global reputation and has begun to criminalize the bribery of foreign officials or officials of international public organizations. This was a necessary step as China's FDI outflows are rapidly growing but the country is ranked 27 out of 28 countries considered in TI's latest 2011 Bribe Payers Index.[1]

[1] Transparency International Brib Payer's Index, 2011 (http://bpi.transparency.org).

© Springer International Publishing Switzerland 2015

H.R. Randau, O. Medinskaya, *China Business 2.0*, Management for Professionals,
DOI 10.1007/978-3-319-07677-5_21

Table 21.1 Transparency International corruption index: major economies

Country	2012 Index (1–10)	World ranking (according to index)
Russia	2.8	127
China	4.0	80
Brazil	4.2	72
USA	7.3	19
Japan	7.4	18
Germany	7.8	12

Transparency International compiles a yearly corruption index, which combines the rankings of 13 surveys from 10 private institutions (including the World Bank and the Economic Intelligence Unit), assigning them a standardized score from 1 (most corrupt) to 10 (least corrupt)

China does not have any independent anti-corruption agencies. Paradoxically, the main anti-corruption body, The Central Committee for Discipline Inspection (CCDI)—which is responsible for ensuring integrity among CCP cadres—is a faction of the CCP itself. The National Bureau of Corruption Prevention (NBCP) is an additional government anti-corruption bureau intended to make China's legal system comply with the United Nations Convention against Corruption. However, it is not authorized to make investigations into individual cases. Hence, Global Integrity 2011 has assessed China's anti-corruption agency as 'weak'.

As gift-giving remains common in China it has become clear that small gifts are normally acceptable. Each agency might have its own internal rules regarding the receipt of gifts by its officials. Gifts of cash, securities, or property to public officials and SOE employees[2] are strictly prohibited. Under the Criminal Law, Chinese officials who receive gifts in excess of Yuan 200 are required to turn the gifts over to their supervisors. The Chinese government has also started to regulate gifts cards: all officials are now strictly prohibited from accepting any kind of gift cards during their official activities.

[2] According to the USA's FCPA Compliance Regulations, gifts to SOE employees are illegal, as they are considered state officials. This may or may not be the case with other nations and internally in China.

INSIGHT: Chris Torrens, Control Risks

Compliance for supply chain networks: adopting the "risk-based" approach to due diligence

While the U.S. Foreign Corrupt Practices Act (FCPA) and UK Bribery Act (UKBA) cover several areas of non-compliance (such as corporate hospitality, gifts and entertainment and political lobbying), global multinationals have learnt the hard way that the greatest integrity risk to their businesses stems from third parties. These "associated parties" (APs) comprise suppliers, vendors, intermediaries, service firms, subsidiaries - in short, pretty much every organization linked to their company. Major multinational companies with global supply chain networks may have tens of thousands of APs. How to achieve and demonstrate compliance across all these organizations?

The answer lies in a risk-based approach to due diligence that underpins the development and maintenance of effective compliance programs. These typically begin with an integrity risk assessment that essentially gauges the level of corruption risk posed by types of APs in relation to the parent company. Key factors include: country of operation, industry type, transaction type, class of partner (including state-owned or private) and importance of relationship. Such categorization and segmentation, while sometimes a little simplistic, creates a manageable compliance framework and helps the parent company to focus on potential vulnerabilities in their operating networks. This process of selection allows for targeted use of time and resources in addressing anti-corruption compliance.

A standard risk-based due diligence program might comprise the following stages:

Step 1: Assign a "risk score" to each of the third parties, based on the nature of relationship, transaction value, ownership, industry sector and track history etc.

Step 2: Conduct different levels of due diligence based on the risk score

- Level 1: Red flag checks on third parties with LOW risk score
- Level 2: Extensive public record checks on ones with MEDIUM risk score
- Level 3: In-depth investigation, including public record research,

interviews, site visits and discreet enquiries, on ones with HIGH risk score

Step 3: A report with a risk rating chart on each of the third parties. Categories of risk could include: political exposure; corruption and bribery; serious and organized crime; money laundering; corporate fraud and financial regulatory breaches; intellectual property violations; civil litigation; and other risk factors.

Third-party risk in China depends to a great extent on understanding the nature of the business relationship - and the potential existence of related party transactions, since the historical development of family business networks is part of China's - and Asia's - success story. Multinationals need to ensure that their staff are totally transparent in declaring any family relationships they have with employees in third-party networks: all too often a sales manager is found to be using a marketing agency, retailer or distribution business owned by a brother, sister or mother-in-law. Such links are a major no-no under the FCPA and UKBA. Only by requiring new staff to read, understand and sign codes of conduct can employers minimize the reputational fall-out and mitigate fraud risk arising from related party transactions - and this process should be repeated every 18 months to two years.

TIPS, OPPORTUNITIES and WARNINGS

Warning: Strict law enforcement for foreign companies

In general, foreign companies must be prepared to meet higher standards than those of local businesses in China in regard to compliance with all regulations, including those dealing with corruption.

The media also tends to be more critical of and outspoken against foreign companies. The violation of corruption laws risks a good reputation.

Tip: Monitor and control your business partners

Managers need to be aware that business partners (e.g. in Joint ventures) can be a risk to the business's reputation. Monitoring their behavior and communicating clear expectations are essential in preventing problems.

Suggestions for Further Reading

Transparency International: The Global Coalition against Corruption	www.transparency.org

Be Aware: Fraud Risks 22

China is constantly plagued by fraud scandals. Anyone, whether only doing business with Chinese companies, managing a subsidiary, seeking investment opportunities or conducting merger and acquisition possibilities needs to be aware of China's high fraud risks. The strong focus on family well-being, the urge to gain status through accumulation of wealth quickly (Chap. 46), weak controls and a generally relaxed attitude to fraud seem to drive such actions. Not surprisingly, Chinese pay great attention to building trust in business relationships and checking the partner's credibility thoroughly.

The main risks can be categorized in four areas: low integrity, corruption, misrepresented finances and the misappropriation of company assets (see Fig. 22.1).

Managing fraud risks is certainly not an easy task. Even basic integrity reviews may prove difficult. As simple a task as the identification of company owners and shareholders may already prove a challenge as corporate records are not always available. Without the right connections information is often not accessible.

In many cases family-members or close friends are involved in fraudulent actions. Shell operations are set up to roll over revenues to family members rather than to shareholders or to pump up revenues. A system of subsidies is used to hide or move profits. Made-up invoices, commissions or agency contracts are often used to scam profits.

Accounting irregularities and unreliable audit results remain another major concern. Some companies operate with different sets of financials, others use fake bank statements. Internal book-keeping practices may differ greatly from western standards, with many local companies operating without a standard costing system.

"Policy loans" are another risk area as the state, no matter whether on a central or a provincial level, is always looking for active ways to expand their local economies. As a consequence, strategic industries and companies with good government-relationships are heavily subsidized. Companies may receive loans at low rates or do not even have to pay back these loans. It is not rare for special loans

© Springer International Publishing Switzerland 2015
H.R. Randau, O. Medinskaya, *China Business 2.0*, Management for Professionals,
DOI 10.1007/978-3-319-07677-5_22

Fig. 22.1 Fraud risks

to remain unaccounted for. These off-balance sheet loans are then counted as profits or used for corruptive actions.

The list of potential irregularities and fraud risks is long and Fig. 22.2 displays further examples. Managers should carefully study auditor reports but are advised to do their own due diligence. Especially in-bound M & A transactions require always a detailed forensic due diligence.

TIPS, OPPORTUNITIES and WARNINGS

Warning: Relationships pose a high integrity risk

The lack of integrity remains a major risk in China. Chinese people are often loyal to their families and people with whom they have built deep bonds (*guanxi*). This tendency has often led to employees becoming more loyal to their personal relationships than to their employers. Even though such a tendency has weakened according to our observations, it still poses a high integrity risk that needs to be closely controlled.

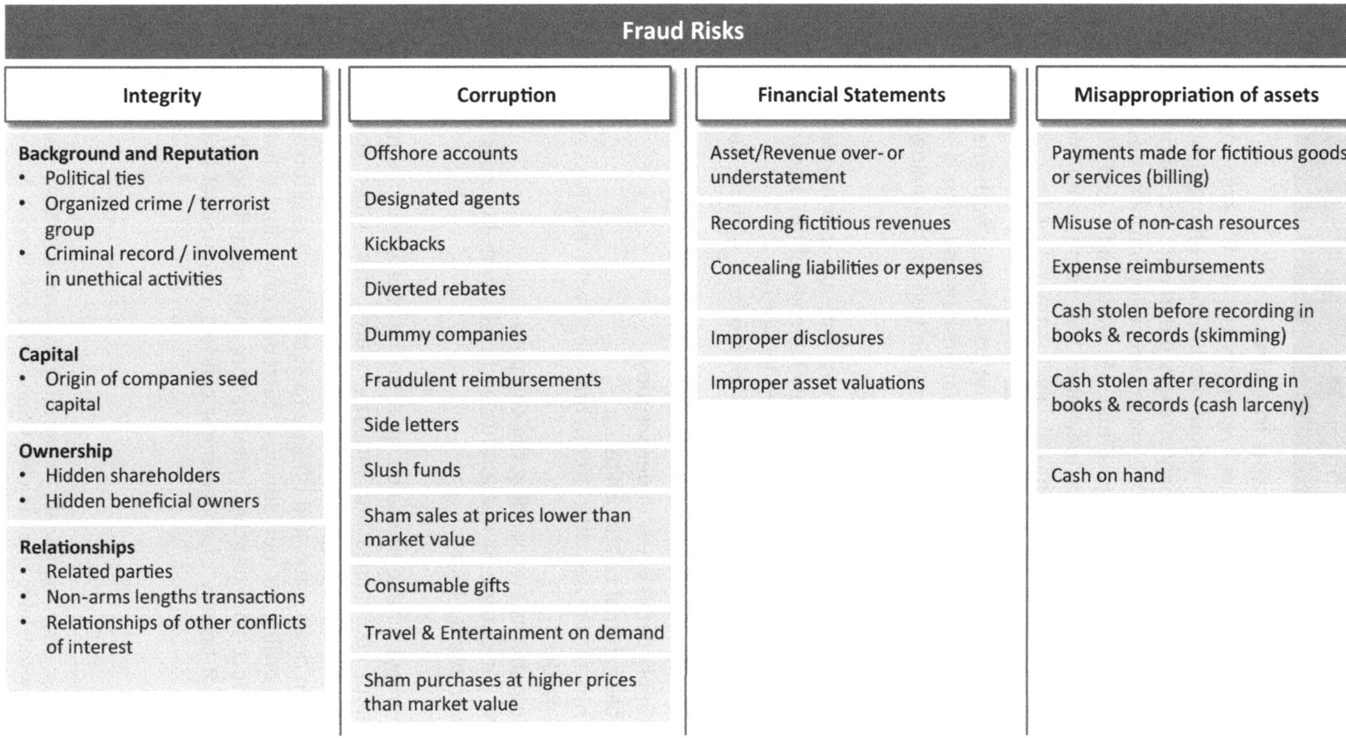

Fig. 22.2 Samples of fraud risks. *Source*: Based on an overview of fraud risks provided by Deloitte with kind permission

INSIGHT: Belinda Tan, Deloitte

(1) Common Red Flags of Fraud in China

Despite the efforts of the Chinese government and increasing public complaints, fraud and graft remain ubiquitous practices amongst businesses in China. Chinese culture increasingly stresses the importance of protecting financial status (Chap. 46) (Allen 2012) and maintaining business ties that are forged upon favorable relationships (Chap. 46) (Kate and David 2006). It is therefore unfortunate, but perhaps inevitable, that some companies resort to bribery, especially of government officials, to attain their financial goals.

When assessing the risk that a business partner or a target has or is involved in dubious activities, it is important to consider both the internal (governance and controls) and external (relationships and clients). Red flags of questionable practices include, but are not limited to, the following:

- Poor corporate governance and controls:
  - no interest or knowledge of government anti-corruption measures
  - few key decision makers and a lack of challenge of decisions
  - large disbursements for entertainment expenses
  - expenses with no apparent business purpose or without supporting documentation;
  - management information lacks detail and employees generally unwilling to supply detail when under scrutiny
- Questionable external relationships:
  - family run businesses that frequently deal with businesses run by related parties
  - negative publicity surrounding the company
  - frequent patronizing of restaurants and clubs with business partners and government officials

Deloitte surveys[1] have revealed that many executives remain very concerned about compliance and integrity-related risks when conducting business in China. Worryingly these concerns appear justified as many M&A transaction deals are called off due to such risks. It is often surprising to see that according to our surveys, currently only about half of the companies conduct an extensive investigation with regards to these risks (e.g. possibility of bribery of government officials, commercial bribery and

(continued)

[1] *Look before you leap - navigating risks in emerging markets*. (2012, August 11). Retrieved from http://www.deloitte.com/view/en_US/us/Services/Financial-Advisory-Services/ccfa48c71d29a310VgnVCM2000003356f70aRCRD.htm

kickbacks, etc.). This is even more surprising as the increasing interest from regulatory bodies such as the Securities and Exchange Commission (SEC), Department of Justice (DoJ) and UK Serious Fraud Office (SFO) compounds the need to tread carefully (Carlson 2012).

(2) Forensic Due Diligence

Traditionally, M&A due diligence has focused on financial performance, position and tax. However, given the fraud, integrity and corruption risks that are more prevalent in emerging markets, it pays to conduct enhanced or forensic due diligence.

A typical forensic due diligence will encompass an analysis of the company's risks in the areas of fraud, bribery and corruption, related-party transactions, conflicts of interest and regulatory exposure. This normally involves a two-pronged approach of analyzing the effectiveness of anti-corruption policies of the business as well as assessing risk exposure from revenue streams and disbursements.

Elements of a Forensic Due Diligence:

- Analyzing effectiveness of anti-corruption measures, ranging from company culture, tone at the top, existing policies and procedures
- Assessing risk exposure to violations from revenue (e.g. fictitious revenue schemes) and expenses (e.g. entertainment of foreign officials)

Forensic due diligence usually results in a stronger negotiating position, e.g. identifying the need for specific warranties or indemnities, but more importantly helps identify those warning signs that may suggest a deal is not worth the trouble. The last thing any firm wants after completing a major deal is to receive regulatory fines, reputational damage or to find themselves beholden to a landlord, supplier, customer or local official who wants a piece of the action.

Suggestions for Further Reading

China Briefing	www.china-briefing.com
China IPR SME Helpdesk	www.china-iprhelpdesk.eu
Deloitte	www.deloitte.com
Ernst & Young	www.ey.com
Legislative Affairs Office of the State Council	www.chinalaw.gov.cn
Ching, M. K. (2009). *CFO guide to doing business in China*. Singapore: Wiley.	
Li, J., & Steininger R. C. (2010). *Steuerstandort China: Praktisches Steuerrecht fuer auslaendische Unternehmen in der VR China*. Wiesbaden: Gabler.	

References

Allen, J. (2012). *Guanxi, mianzi, and business: The impact of culture on corporate governance in china*. World Bank. Retrieved from International Finance Corporation Web site http://www1.ifc.org/wps/wcm/connect/aeae62804b7321708fcdcfbbd578891b/IFCPSO 26 052112.pdf?MOD=AJPERES

Carlson, E. (2012). *Trends and developments in anti-corruption enforcement*. Retrieved from http://www.cov.com/files/Publication/ee200192-e711-47dc-8cd5-15bcaf4bd1f1/Presentation/PublicationAttachment/d362277c-d835-43e0-93fc-183a0f809dae/Trends_and_Developments_in_Anti-Corruption_Enforcement.pdf

Kate, H., & David, W. (2006). Understanding networking in china and the Arab world: Lessons for international managers. *Journal of European Industrial Training, 30*(4), 272–290. Retrieved from http://www98.griffith.edu.au/dspace/bitstream/handle/10072/33699/63895_1.pdf.

A Snapshot on Mass Media

23

China's media structure is becoming exponentially more diverse as it continues to undergo a process of rapid commercialization. Through the increasing number of mobile phone users, the Internet and mobile media are growing especially quickly, with the Internet being key forefront in the fight over public opinion.

23.1 Print Media

According to government reports, print media is booming and the number of publications has soared. Most of these publications are apolitical media belonging to the "yellow press" but tightly controlled by the government. Foreign newspapers sell only selectively in first class hotels in major cities. On the black market, however, thousands of printing houses produce and sell nonofficial material—mostly romance literature and pornography but also political and intellectual journals.

23.2 TV and Radio

Television is a popular source for news and entertainment with a penetration rate close to 100 %.[1] The Chinese spend on average 3 h per day watching TV, with affluent young employees running multiple televisions whenever they are home.

There are more than 2,000 provincial and local TV channels and 3,000 cable channels in the mainland. Foreign broadcasters wishing to air programs in China must pass through strict censorship, with their programs blocked out when controversial. Many foreign TV Shows (such as "Gossip Girl" or "The Vampire Diaries") are not authorized in China and their videos are also removed from websites.

[1] China Statistical Yearbook (www.stats.gov.cn/tjsj/ndsj/2012/indexeh.htm).

© Springer International Publishing Switzerland 2015

H.R. Randau, O. Medinskaya, *China Business 2.0*, Management for Professionals,
DOI 10.1007/978-3-319-07677-5_23

Exceptions include Hong Kong's channels in Guangdong and hotels with international clientele.

The number of radio programs is also strongly growing, climbing from 93 radio stations in 1978 to around 3,000 today.

23.3 Internet and Social Networking

Internet usage is soaring in China, and the country now has the largest user base in the world. The Internet market is dominated by domestic equivalents of popular western websites which are expanding rapidly, including the Chinese search engine Baidu, which held a domestic market share of 78.3 % as of 2012 (compared to Google's 19.6 %) (Fig. 23.1).[2] Few of China's websites link outside the country.

The Chinese love to shop and connect with others on the Internet. Popular social media networks such as Qzone, Sina, Weibo, and Renren have grown exponentially. Users spend an average of 46 min per day on these sites, vs. 7 min in Japan and 37 min in the U.S. One major difference between Chinese and western social

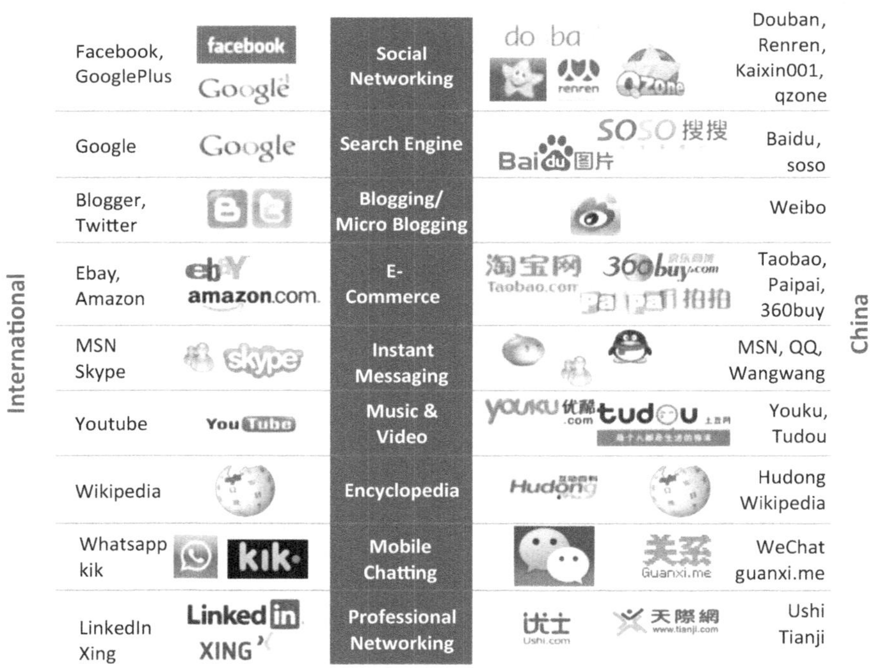

Fig. 23.1 Comparison of Chinese and international websites

[2] South China Morning Post (www.scmp.com).

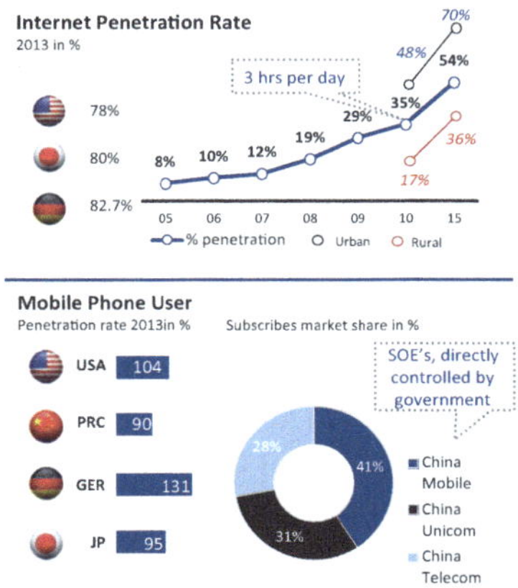

Most popular print media for foreigners in China:

- Far Eastern Economic Review
- Asian Wall Street Journal
- South China Morning Post

Most popular print media:

Renmin Ribao (People's Daily)	The paper of the CPC Central Committee (policy, economy)
Guangming Ribao (Guangming Daily)	Conservative paper,close to the CPC (policy, economy)
Xinmin Wanbao (Shanghai evening news)	Daily paper
Beijing Wanbao (Beijing evening news)	Daily paper
Nan Fang Zhou Mo (South Weekend)	Weekly paper from Guangzhou
Economic Daily	Economy
Jiefangjun Bao (PLA's Daily)	Official daily oft he People's Liberation Army
Beijing Ribao (Beijing Daily)	National daily
China Youth Daily	Paper of Communist Youth League of China
Global Times	Traditional propagandist Communist paper
The China Daily	Official state-run English-language Chinese newspaper
Shanghai Daily	English-language voice of the Shanghai People's Government

Fig. 23.2 Popular media in China. *Sources*: Reuters, Boston Consulting Group, Wirtschaftswoche

networking communities is that the Westerners know each other in "real life", while Chinese networking is often a place to meet strangers rather than contact friends. Criticizing the party and discussing politics has shifted primarily to the social networks. In the future the Chinese leadership will be even more challenged on how it manages to maintain control (Fig. 23.2).

Chinese are also very willing to shop online and E-shoppers in China are greatly influenced by social media in their online purchasing decisions.

TIPS, OPPORTUNITIES and WARNINGS

Warning: Media statistics are often unreliable

Media statistics such as audience and circulation strength are prone to manipulation and can often be unreliable. Most of these statistics are reported by the government, which heavily monitors Internet traffic and by law owns a majority share in all television companies. What is certain is that mobile and Internet media are growing at exponential rates.

23.4 Control and Censorship

Even though the process of commercialization has seen China's press autonomy increase, today foreign investors are still prohibited from setting up or running news organizations. In radio and television networks, a Chinese partner must hold a controlling stake in the production and distribution of the media. This has led to many joint ventures comprising 49 % foreign investment, but where Chinese themes are prerequisite in any programs.[3] Since the majority of any television company must be state-owned, media statistics such as audience and circulation strength are highly unreliable.

China's constitution affords its citizens freedom of speech and press, but Chinese law includes several other regulations with vague language. These regulations provide wiggle room for authorities to, if desired, execute effective control over the media. Even though media has become more autonomous, with news covering accidents, financial scandals, social, and ecological problems, and official wrongdoing, the press in mainland China remains party-controlled. The watchdog group Reporters Without Borders ranked China in its 2013 report 173 out of 179 countries in its worldwide index of press freedom. Reporting limitations mostly pertain to politically sensitive topics: the legitimacy of the Communist Party, riots, independence movements in autonomous regions, Taiwan's government and independence, freedom and democracy, police brutality, obscenity, and pornography.

Systematic control of news within, entering, and exiting China is executed by more than a dozen regulatory bodies. Censorship is applicable only to mainland China, with the SAR's of Hong Kong and Macau having separate media regulatory bodies. The most powerful mainland monitoring body is the CCP's Central Propaganda Department (CPD), which coordinates with General Administration of Press and Publication (GAPP), State Administration of Radio, Film, and Television (SARFT), and the Ministry of Information Industry to ensure content control. The CPD publishes weekly guidelines and enforces these through directives issued to heads of media outlets, demanding that they kill controversial stories and telling them how to cover delicate topics. On top of such national restrictions, provincial and local officials release their own directives.

Television broadcasting is controlled by China Central Television (CCTV), the country's only national network. CCTV's principal directors and other officers are appointed by the State. Chinese news media are required to secure their news sources through Xinhua, a state agency controlled by the propaganda department which censors and edits foreign news. The Chinese government also exercises power over the media market through ownership of all major media production companies including publishing houses, television and radio stations, Internet networks, and ISPs.

The major challenge for the leadership will be how it intends to shape the public opinion as the Internet becomes more and more important in Chinese society. The government has intensified attacks on online media and has made several attempts to "clean up" the Internet. But the authorities face the problem that people are quickly changing their social networks as soon as they become aware of such initiatives. It remains to be seen how the leadership will seek to maintain its censorship regime of the Internet in the future.

---

[3] Beijing Loosens Some Foreign Ownership Limits, 04.01.2012, can be found at: http://online.wsj.com

Suggestions for Further Reading

China Daily	www.chinadaily.com
Chinese State News Agency Xinhua (has the power to censor and edit the news of foreign agencies)	www.xinhuanet.com
South China Morning Post	www.scmp.com

Part III

Doing Business

This part of the book highlights critical hard and soft aspects of doing business in China, centering around finance, taxation, and human resources. The chapters focusing on finance and taxation will familiarize you with the regulatory environment in which businesses need to operate. You may be familiar with some of these concepts and frameworks because the PRC has adopted many international standards, beginning in the 1990s. However, the major difference between the PRC and western countries remains the high complexity deriving from China's multitude of legislative entities, which are involved in setting and executing regulations.

This part also discusses critical HR-related success factors because Human Capital Management remains one of the 'hot topics' in China. High turnover rates, limited skill sets, and a significant imbalance between the supply and demand of managerial talent are major challenges. We will share ideas regarding finding talent and retaining employees. We will also familiarize you with some "hidden cultural rules" and give you ideas on how to adjust your working style to effectively manage staff.

Understanding Entry Modes 24

When China first opened its economy, foreign investment was limited to *Joint Ventures* with Chinese partners. Later, China's entry to the WTO initiated significant changes for investors and enterprises in the country. Today, foreign investors can enter the market by forming Representative Offices, Wholly Foreign Owned Enterprises, and Joint Ventures. With its implementation of a new *Company Law* in 2006, China promoted flexibility in the foreign and domestic management of companies in the PRC while the latest announcements indicate that the government intends to continue to ease the setting-up requirements. But in general, business establishment in China is still a bureaucratic, complex, and lengthy process which involves contacting numerous local and national departments and translating many documents into Chinese. It remains to be seen how fast the announced reform of the company registration system which lowers the capital registration requirements and facilitates the establishment of an enterprise credit system can improve the situation.

However, the government will continue to play an active role in channeling foreign investment into the country. The Foreign Investment Guidance Catalogue outlines sectors where foreign investment is encouraged, restricted or prohibited. The latest catalogue was published by the National Development and Reform Commission (NDRC) and the Ministry of Commerce (MOFCOM) in at the beginning of 2012.

Since each entry mode requires a different set of regulations it is important to understand the advantages and drawbacks of different types of commercial entities in China. First, one should carefully evaluate the future plans. In many cases simply having a sales representative is enough (Graph 24.1). If forming a legal entity is deemed necessary, one needs to define the precise industry focus, or *scope*, of the business. The *scope* should be sufficiently broad because if a company sets too narrow a *scope*, their operations may be disallowed by Chinese authorities.

The importance of capital for companies entering China cannot be understated. Legal minimum capital requirements are established by law according to the company type, but regional magistrates often have their own specific requirements

© Springer International Publishing Switzerland 2015

H.R. Randau, O. Medinskaya, *China Business 2.0*, Management for Professionals,
DOI 10.1007/978-3-319-07677-5_24

Graph 24.1 Company types

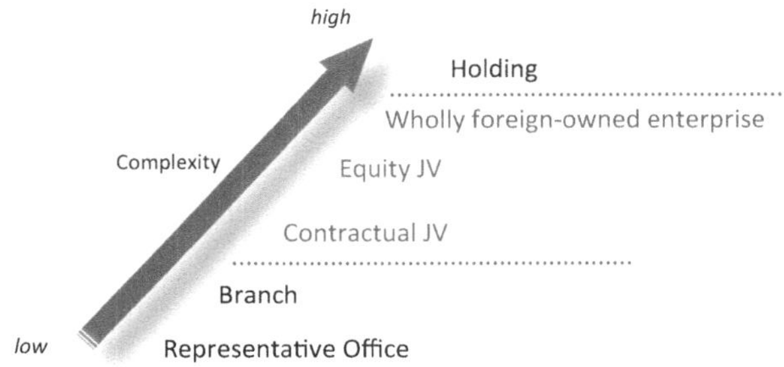

and interpretations. Thus, actual requirements can vary greatly by location and industry. Both the monetary amount of required capital invested on a property and the time elapsed between the acquisition of the property and the building of capital will affect that company's access to land rights, their terms on business loans, and their degree of limited liability in China. Licenses are granted, loans cleared, and operations commenced only after the company's plans for financing are clearly defined, discussed, and approved by the regional government.

The Articles of Association, which relate to business scope, liquidation, total investment, profit repatriation, and trade unions, deserve great attention from foreign managers. According to the Company Law, Articles of Association can be structured to meet the specific needs of each company. Therefore, any potential investor should prepare them in great detail.

Since foreign investors have been permitted to form Wholly Owned Foreign Enterprises, the percentage of total foreign investment allocated to joint venture establishment has fallen. However, for some restricted industries such as media, automobiles and telecom, it is still mandatory for foreign businesses to have local Chinese partners.

Establishing partnerships with local companies, like Joint Ventures, can help companies gain market knowledge and build connections with key authorities, thus providing useful advantages that would be difficult for a foreign enterprise to attain on its own. In past years there has been a trend towards fewer joint ventures. This is not surprising, given the fact that it is difficult to sell shares and exit the constellation. In addition, JVs also bear the risk that one of the partners may run off with the other's know-how (Table 24.1).

Suggestions for Further Reading

China Briefing	www.china-briefing.com
The U.S.-China Business Council	www.uschina.org
U.S. Commercial Service	www.export.gov/china

Table 24.1 Overview of legal entity types

	Representative office (RO)	Cooperative joint venture (CJV)	Equity Joint venture (EJV)	Wholly foreign owned enterprise (WFOE)	Joint stock company (JSC)
Key feature	Office representing parent company; not an independent company	Sino-foreign partnership, profits/losses and ownership shared on a contractual agreement	Sino-foreign partnership, with profits/losses and ownership shared in equal proportion to the equities	Company wholly owned by foreign investor(s)	Ownership of the company is divided into shares like any public corporation
Status	Non-legal person, liabilities extend to parent company	Limited liability or non-legal person (subject to full civil liability)	Legal person, limited liability	Legal person, limited liability	Legal person, limited liability
Number of owners	None	Minimum two of which one must be a Chinese national	Minimum two of which one must be a Chinese national	Minimum of one	At least five promoters; the majority must be domiciled within China
Governance	Chief representative	Board of directors or joint management committee, minimum three	Board of directors, minimum three	Managing director or board of directors, minimum three	5–19 directors. Supervisory committee required
Distribution of profits and losses	May conduct 'liaison' activities for the company; no profit making activities permitted[a]	Profits and losses for each partner divvied according to the terms of the contract	Liability is limited and profits are distributed according to the proportion of equity	All profits and losses borne by parent foreign company	Liability is limited and profits are distributed according to the proportion of equity
Audit	Required	Required	Required	Required	Required
Minimum capital	No capital requirement	China will relax the thresholds of minimum registered capital for the establishment of CJVs, EJVs, WFOEs, and JSCs. Please follow the announcements of China's State Administration of Industry and Commerce (SAIC) to understand the current status			
Pros	Quickest to set up Lowest risk opportunity for initial market testing	Cooperation, responsibility sharing Ideal for short-term projects	Responsibility and risks shared in proportion to the equity with partners	Independence and autonomy of foreign management	Shares are transferable without permission from the other shareholders or authorities

(continued)

Table 24.1 (continued)

	Representative office (RO)	Cooperative joint venture (CJV)	Equity Joint venture (EJV)	Wholly foreign owned enterprise (WFOE)	Joint stock company (JSC)
		Flexible share distribution contract	Flexible share distribution contract	Protection of IPR Simple approval procedure	
Cons	Cannot engage in direct business activities or enter into contracts Must engage local agent to hire staff	General partnership risks Risk of IPR violations Limited equity and management control CJVs without legal person status subject contributing parties to full civil liability	General partnership risks Risk of IPR violation Limited equity and management control	Lack of Chinese insight and local contacts Limited access to government support WFOEs are prohibited in some industries	Complex approval procedure Restrictions on capital increases, statutory reserves, and level of public disclosure

[a]"Liaison activities" include: market research, promoting the represented firm, coordinating foreign business activities, other non-profit generating activities

25 China's Tax Structure

Since 1994 when China implemented its first national tax law, the PRC has made much progress in building its taxation system. In 1994, the law was 6 pages long; since then the government has issued multiple directives, making the system increasingly complex and—as in other countries—ever-changing. The latest milestone in this process was the introduction of the Enterprise Income Tax Law (EITL) reform in 2008: For the first time, domestic and foreign companies are combined under one law.

25.1 Tax Legislation and Administration

The Chinese tax system is unified, with laws formulated at the state level through the National People's Congress.[1] These rules contain mainly general provisions while actual tax legislation is regulated by the MoF and the State Administration of Taxation. Only certain local tax regulations and rules may be formulated at provincial level. Generally the Chinese Tax Administration and legislation consists of following institutions (Fig. 25.1).

25.2 Execution and Interpretation

The sophistication of the Chinese tax system has significantly improved in recent years. The main driver was the need to align with international practices due to countries interweaving with foreign companies.

Enforcement has also tightened, especially for large-scale operations and/or publicly listed companies which are subject to regular tax inspections. Still, Chinese tax laws are subject to a wide degree of interpretation. The same regulations

[1] The SARs do not belong to the system of the PRC.

© Springer International Publishing Switzerland 2015

H.R. Randau, O. Medinskaya, *China Business 2.0*, Management for Professionals,
DOI 10.1007/978-3-319-07677-5_25

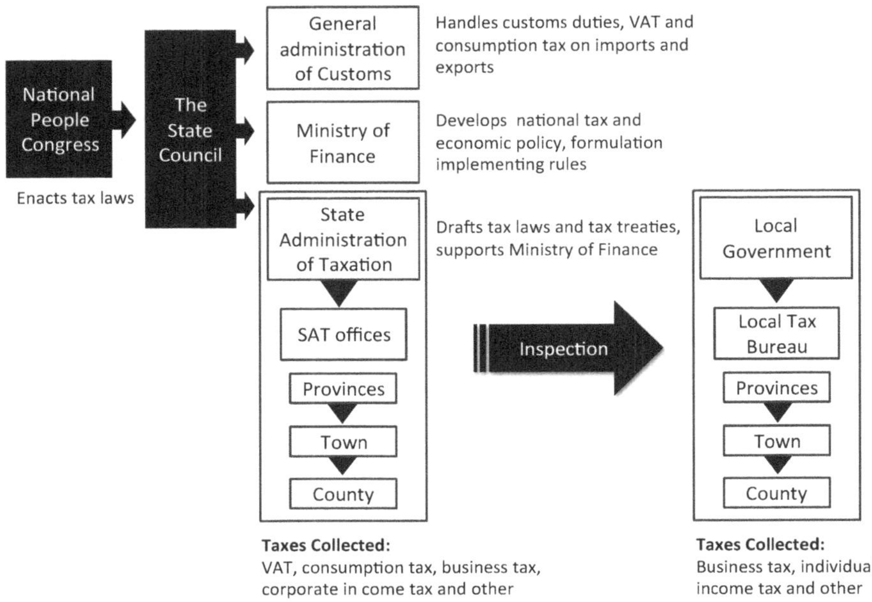

Fig. 25.1 Tax administration institutions

may be implemented in different ways, even in different parts of the same city. Overall, district offices of the State Tax Bureau have a substantial amount of flexibility in interpreting laws, making negotiations between the taxpayer and the tax bureau still essential.

The authorities have also expanded their jurisdiction and investigation in several areas such as tax residency, business purpose, and permanent establishment. They will most likely continue to strengthen their efforts on tax collection by strengthening commercial substance and expanding their focus on topics such as transfer pricing administration.

Even with Chinese tax authorities entering into a stage of maturity, there is still much room for improvement. The system will certainly undergo continuous changes and reorientations in the coming years, e.g. in regard to tax types (new VAT, potential inheritance tax etc.), treaties or in administration and collection rules.

25.3 Tax Treaties

Many foreign countries[2] worldwide have signed double tax agreements (DTAs) with China and its Special Administrative Regions of Hong Kong and Macau.

[2] 2012: 97 countries.

TIPS, OPPORTUNITIES and WARNINGS

Tip: Understand the local authorities' interpretation of tax policies

In China you will be challenged with numerous regulations that can be ambiguous and contradictory. Sometimes rules are not even published at all. Policies remain quite flexible, and because multiple agencies or regulators govern tax law implementation, it is difficult to stay up to date. Keep in close contact with local tax authorities in order to understand their interpretation and approaches to new regulations or additional amendments.

Types of Taxes 26

The Chinese tax system consists of central taxes, local taxes, and taxes shared by the central and local governments. Customs, consumption and income tax revenues collected from SOEs are routed to the central government, while Value Added Tax (VAT) (75 % state, 25 % local) and individual and Enterprise Income Tax (EIT) (60 % state, 40 % local) are split.

There are currently 26 types of taxes, which, according to their nature and function, can be divided into the following categories (Table 26.1).

26.1 Registration

Once approved by the Ministry of Commerce, a business entity is not automatically registered with the tax authority. Therefore, it is necessary to register for tax at the local tax bureau. Additionally, tax certificates must be submitted and confirmed by the tax officer in charge, who determines the types of taxes and the tax rates applicable to the entity.

26.2 Tax Incentives

For several years, China attracted foreign investments by offering tax incentives, such as reduced tax rates or tax holiday periods. However, since the implementation of the Corporate Tax Reform, most tax preferential treatments have been abolished.

Tax benefits and preferences are generally based on China's economic objectives. Companies operating in the high technology, environmental friendly or industrially safe products sector can still receive tax incentives. A company's investment density, export share, and emphasis on advanced technology all figure largely into the tax benefits available to it.

© Springer International Publishing Switzerland 2015
H.R. Randau, O. Medinskaya, *China Business 2.0*, Management for Professionals,
DOI 10.1007/978-3-319-07677-5_26

Table 26.1 Tax groups

1. Business taxation	
• Enterprise income tax (EIT)	
2. Withholding tax	
• Taxes on dividends, interest, royalty	
• Wage tax (the employer must withhold Individual Income Tax on behalf of the employee and remit it to the tax authorities)	
• Social Security (the employer and employee are required to contribute a certain percentage of monthly salary to the social security fund. The total employer contribution can be up to 40 % depending on location)[a]	
3. Indirect taxes	
Turnover tax	• Value-added tax (VAT)
	• Business tax (BT)
	• Consumption tax (CT)
Resource tax	• Resource tax
	• Urban and township land use tax
Special purpose tax	• Urban construction and maintenance tax (UCMT)
	• Education surcharge
	• Land appreciation tax
	• Vehicle purchase tax
Property tax	• House property tax
	• Urban real estate tax
	• Inheritance tax (not yet levied)
Behavior tax	• Vehicle and vessel usage/license plate tax
	• Stamp tax
	• Deed tax
	• Exchange tax (not yet levied)
	• Slaughter tax and banquet tax
Customs duties	Customs duties are imposed on the goods and articles imported into and exported out the PRC
4. Individual taxation	
• Individual income tax (IIT)	
• Agricultural tax levied on the enterprises, units and/or individuals receiving income from agriculture and animal husbandry activities	

[a] *Taxation and Investment in China 2013: Reach, relevance and reliability*, can be found at: www.deloitte.com

Local governments do not have the authority to change tax rates. However, they can offer financial subsidies to foreign investing entities: the entities pay taxes at a normal rate first, but receive a refund from the local government later.

For tax reductions, an application must be submitted to the local tax authority and the Ministry of Commerce.

26.3 Enterprise Income Tax

Certainly the most important corporate tax, the EIT, is levied annually on the profit of an enterprise. Different tax rates apply according to the size and scope of the company.

The EIT rate could be reduced (or tax holidays granted) for qualified enterprises in industries encouraged by the government, such as new or high-tech enterprises. Some foreign companies are reluctant to apply for qualification as a high-tech company, even though it would reduce their tax burden, as it requires them to publish sensitive information or file their patents in China (Table 26.2).

Table 26.2 Overview of enterprise income tax

Levy	On profit of an enterprise
Rate	Standard: 25 % (since 2008 unified for both domestic and foreign) for enterprises and *Representative Offices*
Settlement	Annual, quarterly pre-filing system. The final calculation is based on year-end audit
Administration	Central and local
Formula	IT payable = (Net Income in a financial year − reasonable business cost and loses) × tax rate
Comments	Incentives and privileges: • Different rates for small/low profit enterprises, qualified High-tech Enterprises, and foreign enterprises without permanent establishment in China (see Withholding Tax) • Numerous additional tax incentives for start-up companies and industries of importance (agricultural sector, infrastructure- and environmental protection projects and venture capital)

26.4 Withholding Tax (WHT)

This tax is only relevant if foreign subsidiaries are providing services to China-based businesses. The tax is withheld by the Chinese entity who conducts business with the foreign subsidiary (Table 26.3).

Table 26.3 Overview of withholding tax

Levy	Levied on PRC-derived income of foreign entities and subsidiaries providing services to China-based businesses (e.g. dividends, interest, royalty, rent, etc.)
Rate	10 %, unless there is a tax treaty between China and the foreign country
Settlement	On payment basis
Administration	In-charge tax bureau
Formula	Deducted from gross invoice amount
Comments	Tax is withheld by the Chinese payer. The local entity is the withholding agent and payer of WHT and so has the responsibility of passing the tax to the tax bureau

26.5 Value Added Tax

Chinese companies need to pay a turnover tax, depending on the nature of their business. VAT is imposed mainly on the sales and importation of goods. The general VAT rate is 13 or 17 %. Income is shared between the central and local governments, with the majority going to the central government.

Companies have been allowed to offset the full amount of input VAT (with only a few exceptions) to be credited against its VAT liability, making it a neutral tax. Any small business must pay 3 % of the gross sales amount, which is a simplified VAT calculation without the input VAT credit.

26.5.1 The Golden Tax System

Paper-based invoices created a large black market for counterfeiting and selling illegal invoices. In order to improve the transparency of tax collection and minimize room for falsified invoices, the government launched the so-called Golden Tax Project in the 1990s. It is a multi-functional online platform allowing governmental tax authorities to collect, store, and verify the authenticity of invoices.

The project came about out gradually, and wherever the system was enforced, companies wanting to receive tax reductions had to register with the platform. However, the platform has not yet replaced paper invoices; companies using the system must still distribute original invoices. It is difficult to predict when the PRC will be fully covered by the new, electronic platform.

Invoices, or *fapiaos,* are fundamental for deducting expenses. Every *fapiao* should contain: the countrywide stamp for invoices, the stamp of the company, and the payment amount. Control of invoices is managed by the Tax Bureau. To encourage businesses to use them, major cities have implemented lottery-like scratch fields on *fapiao's*; each *fapiao* offers a potential prize (Table 26.4).

Table 26.4 Overview of value added tax

Levy	Levied on the sale of taxable goods (except intangible assets and real estate), the provision of taxable labor services (processing, repairing, replacement services only), and taxable goods imported into China
Rate	0–17 %. Standard: 17 % for entities with general taxpayer status. Certain necessities (e.g. vegetable oils, gas, coal products for home use, books) taxed at 13 %
Settlement	Monthly
Administration	Collected by the *State Administration of Taxation* (central government), except for VAT on imports which is collected by customs on behalf of tax authorities
Formula	Payable VAT = Input VAT − Output VAT
Comments	Small businesses do not qualify for general taxpayer status. Output VAT is reduced to 3 % but no deductions are allowed on input VAT Export of goods is subject to a zero rated VAT. However, depending on the product category, the refund of previously paid input tax will be reduced and the refund amount subject to a special calculation. The use of a "Customs Handbook" can facilitate the duty and VAT exemption in bonded and processing transaction General taxpayers selling taxable items must issue special VAT invoices to the buyer. In order to do so they must first apply to the tax bureau Usually special invoices are issued through a centrally connected software. Issuing credit notes in this system is rather complicated, as it always requires prior approval by the tax authorities

26.6 Business Tax

The other turnover tax in the PRC is the so-called Business Tax (BT). The income from the BT goes to the local governments and is imposed on services, as long as either the provider or recipient of services is within China. The major difference to VAT is that input VAT paid for the purchase of other goods or services cannot be deducted from BT.

China is currently in the process of replacing BT with VAT. They hope to complete the process by 2015. The service sector will benefit from the unification. The Chinese government hopes that by eliminating the difference in treatment, service companies are encouraged to spend more money on infrastructure and growing their business. A pilot program was launched in 2012 and some service sectors have already been taxed by VAT nationwide since the fall of 2013 (Table 26.5).

Table 26.5 Overview of business tax

Levy	Levied on the turnover of service businesses (e.g. construction, finance, insurance etc.) or entities engaged in the sale of intangible assets or property
Rate	3–20 %. Most services are taxed at 3 or 5 %
Settlement	Monthly
Administration	Tax collected monthly and administrated by the local tax bureau
Formula	BT payable = turnover × tax rate
Comments	Input VAT is not deductible If an entity has different transactions taxable by VAT or BT it will only subject to one or the other (to be determined by authorities) Also applied to foreign entities, regardless of whether it has a permanent establishment in the PRC or not

26.7 Consumption Tax (CT) (Table 26.6)

Table 26.6 Overview of consumption tax

Levy	Form of VAT levied on the production and importation of certain categories of consumable goods (incl. cigarettes, alcohol, jewelry, cosmetics, gasoline and motorcycles)
Rate	Taxes applied to a frequently changing set of goods at a frequently changing rate
Settlement	Monthly
Administration	Collected by the State Administration of Taxation (central government), except for CT on imports which is collected by customs on behalf of tax authorities
Formula	The tax is computed based on sales price and/or sales volume multiplied by the tax rate
Comments	Rates can be over 50 % Consumption tax is often referred to as "luxury tax"

26.8 Other Applicable Corporate Taxes

Other smaller taxes are also of importance to foreign-operated businesses in the PRC. Examples can be found in Table 26.7.

Table 26.7 Overview of other applicable taxes

Stamp tax	Levied on certain documents and contracts (i.e. loan, property, technology, and purchase/sale contracts)
Real estate tax	Imposed on owners, users, or custodians of buildings
Land appreciation tax	Levied on the transaction profits based on the increased value obtained from the transfer of rights to use state-owned land or real estate property
Vehicle license plate tax	Levied on quantity or net-tonnage of motor vehicles

TIPS, OPPORTUNITIES and WARNINGS

Tip: Be aware of changing taxes

Follow the latest publications issued by the Ministry of Finance and the State Administration of Taxation in order to stay up to date regarding the latest reforms of the tax system.

You should closely monitor how the Chinese government is pushing forward its reform of the Business Tax. Pay attention to the input VAT as well, as China has established a system of VAT rebates and exemptions with the intention of encouraging companies to export. However, China's high trade surplus has forced the government to reduce or revoke these exemptions for certain items, resulting in additional costs for exported goods.

INSIGHT: Titus von dem Bongart, Ernst&Young

Overall Tax Situation in China

The tax landscape in China has gone through dramatic changes in the last 10 years. The fast modernization of the Chinese society and economy, the substantial inflow of foreign investment, China's access to the WTO and not least the emergence of its own outward investment orientation has put a lot of strain on the tax administration.

Basically, the applicable rules and regulations are in line with what international companies face in their home – and other major markets, whereas the remaining "China specific" areas have been recently or are currently under transformation to become more aligned to the international tax practice. There is a new Corporate Income Tax law since 2008 and a major overhaul of the turnover tax system started in 2012 with an estimated completion not before 2014. This reform, currently run under the name "VAT – Pilot", is designed to consolidate the major scope of Business Tax into Value Added Tax. Taxation of international holding companies, Transfer Pricing as well as Permanent Establishments are other areas where there have been significant changes to the applicable taxation.

The above reform and changes have been implemented in a comparatively short period of time, thus sometimes not only overwhelming the finance people of foreign investors but also the tax officials on the executing levels which is one of the reasons why, in practice, the administration and processing of tax matters can be challenging.

Going forward, it is foreseeable that the evolvement of the tax landscape will continue. Likely areas of future reforms are the tax administration, a further focus on behavioral taxes, e.g. resource and energy consumption taxes as well as property taxes and a further adjustment of the Individual Income Tax and the treatment of partnerships. At the same time, the continued focus on structures and transactions deemed to be abusive as well as a further tightening of the regular tax administration can be expected. It is worth mentioning that China has started to re-negotiate its double tax treaties with a couple of its trading partners, introducing more favorable conditions for the respective foreign investors, e.g. reduction of the Withholding Tax on dividends. In this regard, China may continue to steer a course in close relation to its overall direction for its society as outlined in the respective five year plans.

Looking at the developments after the opening to foreign investors, China has significantly modernized its tax regime and it is likely that this process will continue. It is, however, also to be expected that the current challenges for tax practitioners like the ununified interpretation of the existing rules will remain.

Suggestions for Further Reading

Deloitte	www.deloitte.com
China Briefing. The China Tax Guide	www.china-briefing.com
Ernst & Young	www.ey.com
Li, J., & Steininger, R. C. (2010). *Steuerstandort China: Praktisches Steuerrecht fuer auslaendische Unternehmen in der VR China*. Wiesbaden: Gabler.	

26.9 Individual Income Tax

The new IIT Law is significantly changing the individual taxation system. With its 7-bracket progressive rates, it may help expand domestic demand. It can also be seen as a first step to tackle income disparity, as it aims mainly at giving tax relief to low and medium income earners. The tax rate for the lowest income bracket was reduced from 5 % to 3 %, while that for the highest income earners increased to 45 % (see Table 26.8).

Table 26.8 Overview of IIT

Levy	Tax on the income of employees. Tax year runs from January to December
Rate	Progressive rates from 3 % up to 45 %
Settlement	Monthly, from 7 to 15 days after month-end. Additional annual self-declaration required for individuals with annual income over 120 kYuan
Administration	Both central and local
Formula	IIT=taxable income × applicable tax rate − quick deduction figure (see Fig. 26.1) Taxable Income = Monthly Salary − allowable deductions
Comments	Tax rates and taxable incomes vary according to employee's position and their duration of their stay in the PRC

26.10 Method of Calculating IIT

The amount of income taxable by the IIT is determined in two steps:

First, all mandatory welfare contributions, such as insurance (medical, employment injury, maternity), unemployment benefits, state pensions, and housing funds are deducted from the gross income. Secondly, a so-called "monthly standard deduction" (MSD) must be subtracted. A further "quick deduction" applies after the progressive tax rate (Fig. 26.1).

26.11 Foreign Individual Taxpayers

China-domiciled individuals (Chinese citizens or foreigners residing for more than 5 consecutive full years) are subject to Individual Income Tax on their worldwide income. International assignees (those residing for under 5 years) coming to work in the PRC are generally liable to Chinese IIT on their PRC sourced income. This means that they are not only liable for IIT on income received from work (employed or self-employed), but are also liable for any interest and rental income earned in the PRC.

Foreign holders of resident permits must register with the tax authorities upon entering PRC. The following graph displays the general rules for taxation of foreigners (Fig. 26.2).

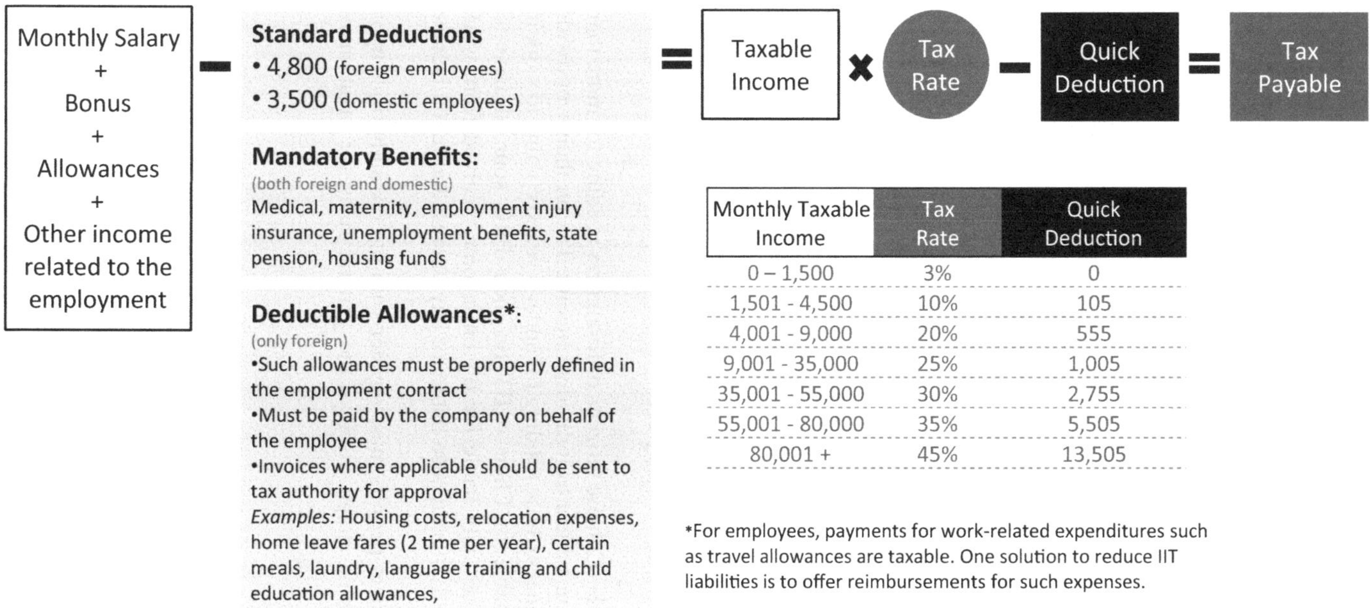

Monthly Taxable Income	Tax Rate	Quick Deduction
0 – 1,500	3%	0
1,501 - 4,500	10%	105
4,001 - 9,000	20%	555
9,001 - 35,000	25%	1,005
35,001 - 55,000	30%	2,755
55,001 - 80,000	35%	5,505
80,001 +	45%	13,505

Fig. 26.1 IIT calculation

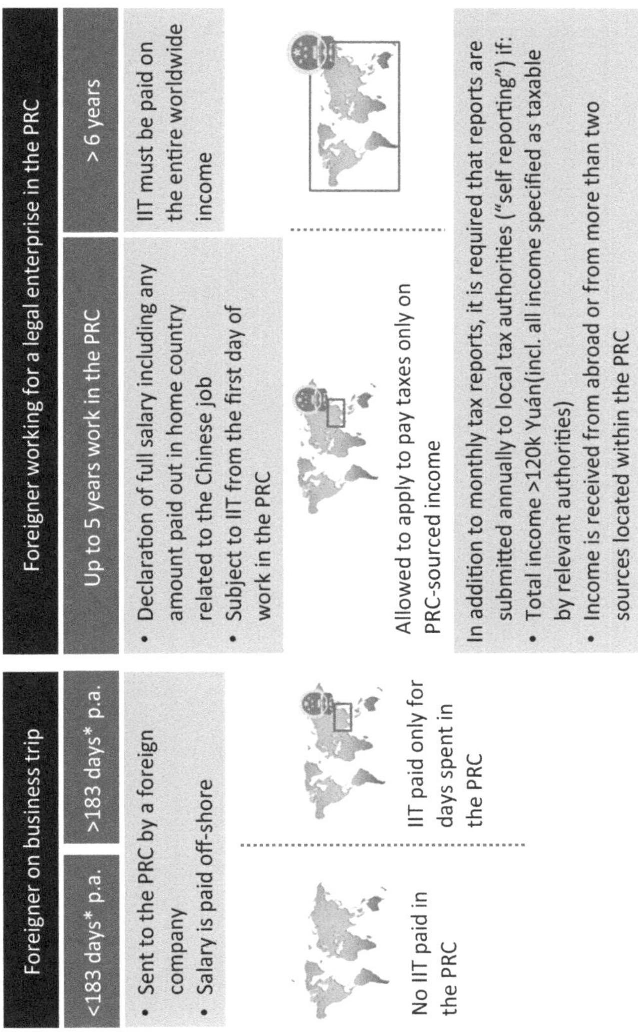

Fig. 26.2 IIT for foreigners in China

27 Passing Audits and Annual Examinations

Chinese regulations require an annual statutory audit by external auditors, who evaluate whether financial statements are fairly presented in accordance with the New Chinese Accounting Standards (CAS) in all material aspects. As usual, the verified accounting income forms the basis for determining the taxable income after the according adjustments.

Audits in China include several unique practices. For example, the Foreign Exchange Audit for Foreign Invested Enterprises (FIEs) reviews foreign currency transactions and is important since the Chinese currency, the Yuan, is not freely convertible. Perhaps the most prominent difference is the Annual Inspection, which is license and certificate renewal. During the Annual Inspection, various administrative authorities inspect whether the company has operated according to the laws and regulations within its *scope* of responsibility as permitted by its PRC business license. Passing the Annual Inspection is as important as a clean auditor's opinion for any company in China as it assures that the company will have its licenses renewed and be able to carry on its business (Table 27.1).

TIPS, OPPORTUNITIES and WARNINGS

Tip: Monitor the changes in the Annual Report System

China's State Administration of Industry and Commerce (SAIC) has announced plans to replace the current annual business inspection system with an annual reporting system, permitting annual reports to be open to public inquiry. The goal of this change is to increase company information transparency in order to protect creditors and the public form fraudulent companies. Please be advised to follow up on the future implementation of such a reporting system.

© Springer International Publishing Switzerland 2015

H.R. Randau, O. Medinskaya, *China Business 2.0*, Management for Professionals,
DOI 10.1007/978-3-319-07677-5_27

Table 27.1 Standardized inspections and audits in China

Accounting and annual statutory audit
• Audit must be conducted by independent Chinese-registered external auditor • Mandatory for all FIEs and joint stock companies • Generally, the Board of Directors of the company is responsible for the appointment, compensation, and oversight of the work of the external auditor • All accounting documents, books, and statements must be prepared in accordance with CAS, must be written in Chinese (and concurrently in a foreign language), and should be recorded in Yuan • Accounting records, general books, and company documents related to the audit must be retained for a minimum of 15 years • The accounting software must be registered by the Ministry of Finance or the local Finance Bureau • Filing with the relevant authorities must be done within four to six months of the following year end, depending on local regulations
Foreign exchange audit
• Required, in concordance with the State Administration of Foreign Exchange (SAFE), for all companies with a foreign exchange account and transactions • Part of the annual statutory audit and carried out by the external auditor
Annual inspection
• Audit results, additional documents, and licenses must be submitted to seven administrative authorities: The Bureau of Foreign Trade and Economic Cooperation, the Administration of Industry and Commerce, the Economic Committee, the Financial Bureau, the State Administration of Taxation, the State Administration of Foreign Exchange, and Chinese Customs • In some provinces, documents can be given to a single administrative agency for a joint Annual Inspection • The separate authorities listed above will each inspect whether the enterprise has conducted business within its *scope* and according to the relevant rules particular to their department. Firms failing the Annual Inspection must then amend their business practices and revise the documents accordingly by the end of April the following year, or risk the revocation of their business licenses

27.1 Financial Statements Under the New CAS

In 2006 the Chinese government issued a new set of accounting standards, commonly known as the New Chinese Accounting Standards. This was an important milestone in China's path towards a globally integrated economy, as the new regulations are substantially in line with IFRS and support the international convergence of accounting standards.

However, the new standards were initially mandatory only for publicly listed companies in Mainland China. Private Chinese enterprises have been encouraged to implement the new CAS but are still allowed to use the old regulations. Thus, there are two parallel sets of accounting standards in China.

The purview of the new CAS will be expanded drastically in the next few years, as it is expected to become mandatory for all medium and large-sized enterprises across the mainland. In most provinces this change has already been implemented, but enforcement depends largely on local authorities.[1] In the future, the adoption of the new CAS will mean great change for many smaller, local companies.

The framework of the new CAS consists of one new Basic Standard, 38 specific Accounting Standards for Business Enterprises (ASBEs) and an implementation guide with interpretations. Most standards are similar to IFRS, except for certain modifications reflecting China's unique business environment. The following tables compare demonstrate the major accounting recognition and measurement differences between IFRS and the new system (Table 27.2):

[1] Status as of July 2012.

Table 27.2 Comparison of IFRS and CAS

Financial statements		
Item	IFRS	New CAS
Accounting year	The start and the end of reporting period is not specified, but statements must be completed at least annually (IAS 1.36)	All companies in China have the same accounting year-end: December 31 (Art. 11 of "*Accounting Law*")
Classification of expenses in income statement	Companies can classify expenses based on either their nature or their function (IAS 1.82, 1.99 and 1.104)	Expenses must be classified based on their function (CAS 30.26; CAS 30.AG IV(VI))
Reporting of cash flows from operating activities	Enterprises can choose between direct and indirect method to present cash flows from operating activities (IAS 7.18)	Both direct and indirect method are required (CAS 31.8 and 16; CAS 31.AG.III (I))
Exemption for parent companies from the obligation of preparing consolidated financial statements	IFRS exempts certain parents from presenting consolidated financial statements if the cumulative conditions of IAS 27 are met	No exemption possible. All parent companies shall prepare consolidated financial statements (CAS 33.13)
Balance sheet and income statement		
Item	IFRS	New PRC GAAP
Investment property	Held by property owner or lessee under financial lease. For subsequent measurement either the cost model or fair value model can be chosen. (IAS 40.5, 40.6 40.30, 40.53)	Held by a property owner or a land use right holder. Subsequent measurement requires the cost model, unless the fair value can be reliably determined on a continuing basis (CAS 3.2, 3.9, 3.10; CAS 3.AG.II; IG of CAS, Section 2.2. Chapter 4)
Intangible assets: Land Use Rights (LUR)	Shall be classified as an operating lease and cannot be revalued unless the land interest is eligible to be classified as investment property (IAS 17.2(a), 17.19, 17.33)	Generally recognized as intangible assets, except for: (1) LUR on built-up land which is accounted as fixed assets together with its buildings and (2) LUR qualified as investment properties (CAS 6.AG.VI)
Subsequent measurement of fixed and Intangible assets	The cost or revaluation model (IAS 16.29 and 38.8, 38.72)	Only the cost model permitted (CAS 4.14-20 and 6.16-21)
Impairment of assets	Only the reversal of impairment loss for goodwill is prohibited (IAS 36.114; IFRS 5.21 and 5.22)	The reversal of all impairment losses is prohibited (CAS 8.17; IG of CAS, Selection 3.1 Chapter 9)
Cost for securing a contract	Direct cost may be allocated to a contract (IAS 11)	Such cost must be expensed as incurred (CAS 15)

INSIGHT: Sheng Tantzscher, Ernst&Young

1) The New Chinese GAAP (CAS)

China's legal environment is maturing, and accounting rules and regulations have greatly improved in recent years. Most new methodologies were introduced through pilot programs. It must be assumed that the pattern of piloting will continue in the future. Thus, pilot activities give a good hint about the future direction.

The adoption of the new Chinese Accounting Standard (CAS) to replace the old PRC GAAP is a logical step towards improved governance and, because of that, unavoidable. However, the Minister of Finance has not issued an official timetable for the adoption of CAS throughout China. The implementation will be executed step by step at the provincial level with different timelines. It must be expected that a simplified version of New Chinese Accounting standards for small-size enterprises will be introduced in the future. It is important for management to monitor the development closely and check whether an early adoption of CAS on a voluntary basis may be a good option to secure a smooth transition.

In the future, the regulatory bodies might also introduce a Fair Value Concept in the new CAS. This would greatly promulgate the development of a valuation market. Currently the assets appraisal market is dominated by local valuation firms. The quality of assets appraisal and valuation needs to be improved to meet international standards.

C-SOX

The expansion of the Chinese capital market required more stringent corporate governance and regulatory oversight. Especially, systematic internal control and risk management has become crucial for Chinese companies to increase trust in the market.

In 2008, several government agencies jointly enacted the Basic Standard of Internal Control for Enterprises (hereinafter called "the Basic Standard"). It is also informally known as C-SOX due to its similarity to the requirements imposed on U.S.-registered public companies under Section 404 of the Sarbanes-Oxley Act of 2002 ("US-SOX").

C-SOX contains 50 articles set out in seven chapters which set requirements over a company's internal control framework. The five key elements are internal environment, risk assessment, control activities, information and communication, and internal monitoring.

The release of the Basic Standard is an important milestone as it demonstrates an increased convergence and integration between the Chinese economy and the global economy. C-SOX took effect on Jan 2011 for Chinese companies listed overseas (e.g. U.S., HK, etc.) and on 1 Jan 2012 for those Chinese companies listed to the main board of domestic stock exchanges (Shanghai/Shenzhen). Large- and medium-sized Chinese companies that are not publicly listed are also encouraged to implement the Basic Standard.

Suggestions for Further Reading

Ching, M. K. (2009). *CFO Guide to doing business in China*. Singapore: Wiley.

28 Protecting Intellectual Property

China's IPR infringement problems are the fodder of popular press. Chinese IP pirates use sophisticated techniques, and can now counterfeit the entire look, feel, and experience of western retail brands like Apple and IKEA (Fig. 28.1).

The concept of IPR is rather new in China. The first major step taken to protect IPR came in the form of a new patent law enacted in 1984. In the subsequent years China adopted several international treaties including the Madrid Trademark Agreement (1989) and the Agreement of Trade Related Aspects of Intellectual Property Rights (TRIPS). Since joining the WTO, China has further strengthened its legal framework, and with a third major revision of the Chinese Patent Law (2008), Chinese IP Laws now officially meet international standards. Most laws are now based upon international treaties, making Chinese IP rights similar to western countries, at least nominally.[1]

Even though the Chinese government is increasingly supportive of IP owners (lately, several big western companies have won IPR cases in court), enforcement remains the major concern. Few Chinese are aware that IPR infringement is a crime, and most people only consider the economic advantages that counterfeiting provides. Fake products have become a major source of income in several regions, and even some SOE's use them. Due to China's large size, uniform enforcement is difficult; corruption and legal protectionism often weaken the strength of central legislation. China has multiplied the number of authorities able to grant and enforce IPR, helping to spread its modernizing policies across China but also complicating the processes surrounding it.

Furthermore, courts throughout the nation, save the Shanghai and Beijing urban centers, lack experience and qualification in dealing with IPR regulations (Table 28.1).

[1] For a detailed comparison of the Chinese and European IPR system please see http://www.china-iprhelpdesk.eu

© Springer International Publishing Switzerland 2015

H.R. Randau, O. Medinskaya, *China Business 2.0*, Management for Professionals,
DOI 10.1007/978-3-319-07677-5_28

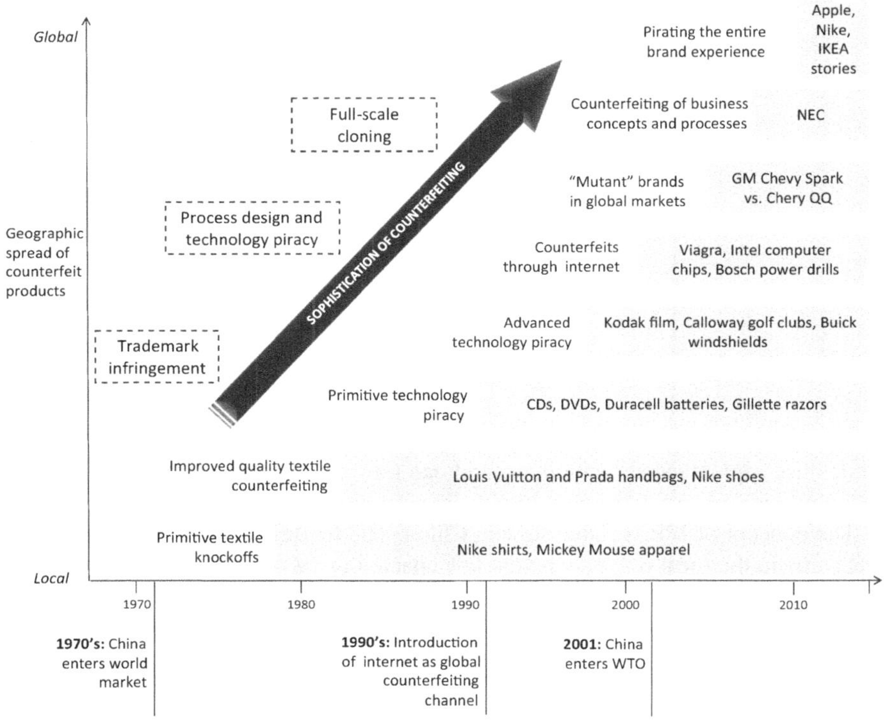

Fig. 28.1 The evolution of counterfeiting. *Source*: Used with kind permission from A.T. Kearney and own illustration

Table 28.1 Comparison of IPR governing bodies

	Name	Task	Additional information
AQSIQ	General Administration of Quality Supervision, Inspection and Quarantine	Supports IPR cases related to quality, health, and safety issues, especially those concerning fake goods with improper labeling	Grants permission to cooperate with a trademark agent or to approach the organization directly
GAC	General Administration of Customs	Supports all types of IPR infringements	Initiated when an IPR holder mentions that an infringing product is about to be exported
NCA	National Copyright Administration	Copyrights	Protects IPR in the fields of art and literature
(S)AIC	(State) Administration for Industry and Commerce	Trademarks	Foreign firms are required to cooperate with a Chinese lawyer or qualified agent
SIPO	State Intellectual Property Office	Patents	Manages the IPR complaint center

Table 28.2 Patent types covered by Chinese law

	Invention	Utility model	Design
Focus	New technical solutions relating to a product or a process	New technical solution relating to the shape, the structure, or their combination, of a product which is fit for practical use	New shape or other visible attributes of a product that is fit for industrial application
Term	20 years term	10 years term	10 years term
Examination aspects	Substantial examination, utility, novelty, inventiveness	Preliminary examination, utility, novelty	Preliminary examination, utility, novelty
Duration of application	3–5 years	1 year	1 year

28.1 Patents

Companies can register three kinds of patents in China: invention, utility, and design patents. Protection for utility models is similar to that for invention patents. The patentability rules for both types are based on three elements: Novelty, inventiveness (lower requirements for utility models), and practical applicability. In order to obtain an enforceable patent as fast as possible, it may be advantageous to apply for a utility model patent and an invention patent at the same time. Once an invention patent is granted, the applicant is free to abandon the utility model patent in favor of the invention patent.

Under China's Patent Law, if two applicants file for identical invention-creation, the patent right will be granted to the applicant whose application was first. This differs from U.S. practice, where decisions are based on the 'first to invent' approach (Table 28.2).

28.2 Trademarks

Trademarks demand major attention. Similar to patent registration, trademarks in China follow a first-to-file system: no matter how long a trademark has been used on international markets, the trademark rights will be granted to the person/company that has filed the application within China first. In order to diminish the risk of a hijacked trademark, it is very important to register within the PRC as soon as possible. China's membership in the Madrid Protocol allows companies to register either through the national Chinese system or through the international system.

China has adopted most parts of the Nice Classification System. Common Chinese goods and services have been added to the system, and subclasses within each of the 45 International Classes are further designated according to the similarity of the goods or services. For maximum protection, one should apply to as many

Table 28.3 Trademark registration overview

	National	International
Organization	China Trademark Office (CTMO)	World Intellectual Property Organization (WIPO)
Duration	Valid for 10 years	Valid for ten years
Application language	Chinese	English, French or Spanish
Agents	Chinese trademark agent must handle the application for foreign applicants	Local trade agent only necessary when China has objections regarding the registration
Classification and fees	International classification of Goods and Services under Nice Agreement (1,000 Yuan per 10 item class, additional item 100 Yuan each)	International classification of Goods and Services under Nice Agreement (fee includes up to three classes)

sub-classes as possible. A separate application must be filed out for each trademark class (Table 28.3).

28.3 Enforcement

IPR owners can tackle infringement problems in China through a variety of paths and organizations.

Foreign companies seeking to enforce their IPR have traditionally relied on customs regulations, primarily due to its perceived lower cost and greater speed. However, with the proliferation of specialized IP tribunals and improvements in the legal system, administrative complaints and legal action are becoming increasingly attractive.

Crucial to IPR enforcement in China is the ability to prove an infringement. Relevant trademarks, patents, and copyrights must be established in China before action to protect them can be taken, and documentation detailing the process must exist in the language spoken in your company and in Chinese. Having IP designations outside the PRC does not guarantee they will be upheld in China.

Administrative complaints are addressed to the Intellectual Property Office (IPO), which investigates disputes and cases. Those deemed serious are passed on to the Ministry of Public Security (MPS), which criminally prosecutes IPR cases through the Economic Crime Investigation Department (ECID) and the Public Security Bureau (PSB). The type of IP one holds determines which enforcing bodies the case will pass through.

Most cases take the administrative route of enforcement, with only serious, evidence supported cases qualifying for criminal and civil prosecution. Alternatively, the Technology and Science Bureau (TSB) has the authority to inspect, seize, and destroy counterfeited or IP-infringing goods through customs regulations. If it encounters serious cases, it too can pass them to civil and criminal courts (Fig. 28.2).

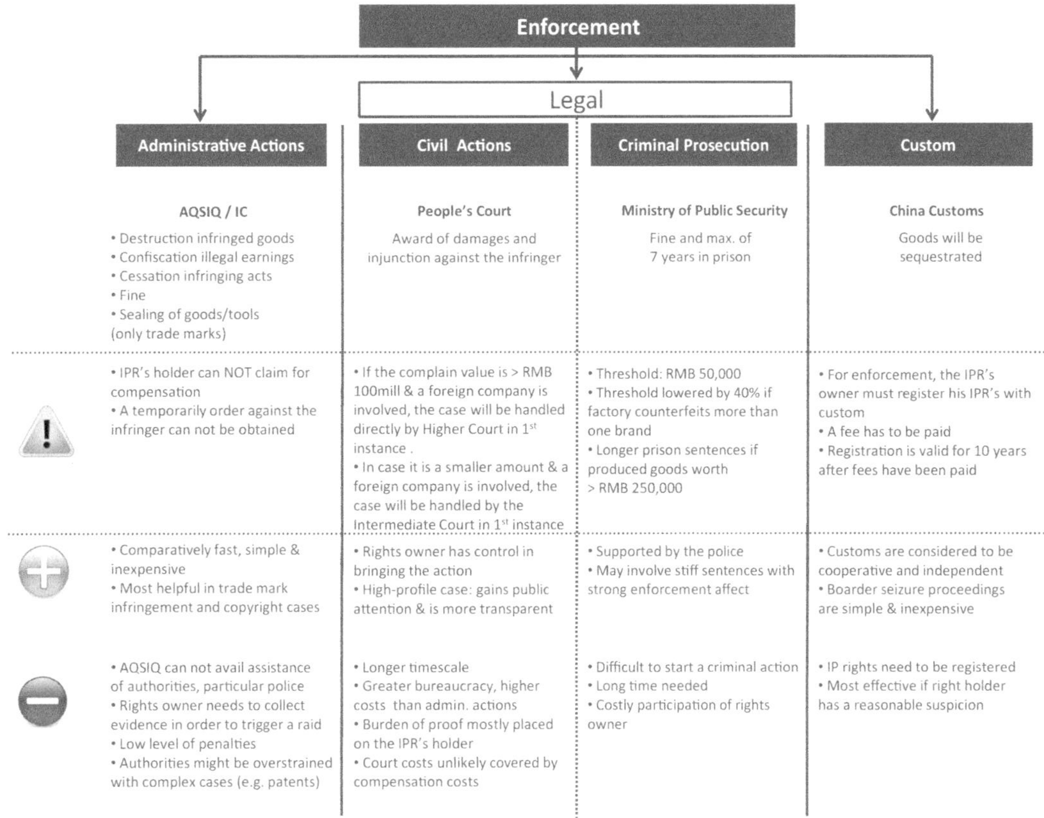

Fig. 28.2 Forms of legal enforcement in China

TIPS, OPPORTUNITIES and WARNINGS

Tip: Seek professional advice to protect your patents and trademarks

Translating patents and trademarks accurately is of utmost importance. If there is no translation of the trademark, its name will neither be protected in Chinese nor in its native language. When granted approval of the application, a rights holder is entitled to use the term 'registered trademark' and other symbols including '®' and the Chinese-character equivalent 注 (*zhù*).

For patents, seek professional confirmation of the translated documents to avoid errors. Otherwise, even a granted patent could be vulnerable to imitations.

INSIGHT: Elliot Papageorgiou, Rouse

How to manage Intellectual Property in China

In essence there are 10 areas of focus when developing an effective China IP strategy:

1. **Register your IP rights in China** – IP rights are national in nature, which means that in order to secure enforceable rights in China, you must file them and get them registered in China. Without your own rights in China, you not only have no redress against someone else taking your intellectual property, you may even lose your own "freedom to operate" (FTO), i.e. to do business, in China!
2. **Keep a watch on local competitors and their rights; invalidate threatening IP rights when appropriate/necessary; secure evidence of "prior use" and "prior art" to protect your FTO** – Everyone is aware of the explosion of IP registrations in China especially by local Chinese companies. It is therefore essential to keep a watch on local filings in your technology space, and when any rights are identified as potential threats, that prompt invalidation is considered. You are the expert in your technology field, so you should keep formalised records of your *prior use* and *prior art*, which can serve to invalidate Chinese IP rights.
3. **Adapt your IP filing strategy for China** – Most companies think of protecting "What I need to do business!" In China it helps to be paranoid and ask "What do I not want others to take away from me?" So filing trade marks to cover related services (e.g. if you produce tyres, then also file trade marks to protect the services associated with fitting tyres/automotive use/repairs etc.) is just common sense for China, as is filing trade marks for packaging and labelling, when your primary marks relate to goods to which such packaging and labelling will apply. As far as patents are concerned, many companies now prioritise Chinese IP filing at the same level as their *'triadic'* filings (patent filings in the US, Japan and EU). Given that China is both one of the world's largest exporters, as well as one of its largest potential markets for numerous products, filing in China should no longer be 'optional'.
4. **Conducting an IP Due-Diligence of new acquisitions and Chinese subsidiaries** is essential – In the heat of an M&A deal, checking for

potential IP 'potholes' or even 'sinkholes' is often low priority. In China it should never be. Not only do many Chinese acquisition targets look more attractive from an IP perspective than they genuinely are (not surprising given the level of 'imi-novative' patents filed in China), but while both local and foreign competitors may also be reluctant to take patent enforcement action against a domestic company, once that company is acquired by an international rival, the situation changes dramatically and 'latent' risks become painfully 'patent'.

5. **A comprehensive HR strategy is core to a strong IP strategy** – Put simply, staff-turnover is in China often a major source of IP loss. This means tuning your HR strategy to reduce employee turnover, keeping a keen eye on the market and 'market price' of your staff, and ensuring that the employment relationship and what follows after it ends has been thoroughly considered and contractually settled.

6. **Investigations are key to IP enforcement** – China has very low levels of required disclosure in legal proceedings. Additionally as there are no judicial safeguards like penalties for perjury or contempt of court, parties can simply refuse to disclose essential information. Investigations of the infringement (and infringer) are therefore almost always the essential first step for IP enforcement.

7. **Recall that China has 3 routes for IP enforcement** – While one of the primary means for enforcing IP in China is, in common with other jurisdictions, by civil litigation, most IP enforcements (by number) are conducted by the administrative authorities. These include the Administration for Industry & Commerce (the AIC – responsible in the case of infringements of trademarks under the trade mark law, and/or acts of unfair competition), the Technology Supervision Bureau (the TSB – dealing with enforcement of various quality laws, and investigating and enforcing against anti-counterfeiting), some of the various Provincial Patent Administrative Bureaux, as well as China Customs. Customs deserves a special mention because not only does Chinese Customs filter imports, like its international counterparts, it also monitors *exports of goods from China*, making Customs recordal and training an excellent investment. Finally, China imposes criminal penalties where *inter alia* certain threshold levels of counterfeiting have been reached, and many rights holders consider criminal penalties

to be the most effective type of enforcement, with the greatest deterrent effect.

8. **The venue of your dispute is crucial** – Not only does IP experience of courts differ substantially across China, so does attitude and aptitude of the courts and judges to the subject of IP law. While courts in Beijing sometimes appear to take a more conservative approach to such matters as judicial review of trade mark or patent office decisions, documentation and compensation, Shanghai courts may be more liberal on the very same subjects. Being forced to issue (or for that matter, forced to respond to) proceedings away from your favourable jurisdiction can make the difference between winning and losing an IP case in China. Databases like www.ciela.cn provide useful (and as mentioned above, often necessary) information about the track record of certain IP tribunals and the outcome of their cases.
9. **Chinese companies are "taking aim" at foreign companies in IP disputes more often** – Before the watershed case of CHINT v. Schneider, modest publicity surrounded IP cases involving foreigners as defendants. However since that case, there has been quite explosive growth in high profile, highly compensatory cases with foreigners as defendants being reported in China. The lesson to be learnt for foreign companies is: never again underestimate Chinese adversaries in IP disputes, or overestimate your own 'hand'. This neatly leads us into our final tenet relating to IP in China.
10. **Effective Intellectual property protection and enforcement is possible in China** – it just requires preparation, vigilance, patience, adaptability to change, and finally a "recalibration" of your expectations.

Suggestions for Further Reading

China IPR SME Helpdesk	www.china-iprhelpdesk.eu
American Chamber of Commerce	www.amchamchina.org

Chinese Migrants: The Hukou System 29

The term *hukou* (pronounced who-koh) refers to China's household-registration system, which defines access to welfare. Required by law since 1958, the system records every Chinese citizen as a permanent resident of a particular city or county. Before 1980, citizens were strictly required to stay in the neighborhood of birth and could not seek employment or education elsewhere in the country.

Dating back to China's ancient 'class-system' permits, the *hukou* system was originally intended to register people and deliver them appropriate social services. A more lenient version of the regulations persists today, requiring any Chinese citizen staying outside of their *hukou* for longer than 3 months to apply for a temporary residency, involving a working contract and extensive paperwork. Rural migrants desiring to relocate to cities still encounter many difficulties including qualifications and contract hurdles.

"Illegal" rural migrants without a temporary permit, are fully in the hands of their employers, receiving low salaries and having no social coverage. While urban residents enjoy guaranteed medical services, education, pensions and other social welfare programs such as subsidized public housing, these illegal workers lack any access to social welfare. Perhaps the most severe consequence of this faulty system is the damage to rural children. Since rural *hukou* holders cannot enroll their kids in urban schools, children are often left behind in villages with the elderly.[1]

These setbacks have done little to hinder migrants from working illegally in the big cities. More than 200 million internal migrant workers are now estimated to live in Chinese cities—many without *hukou*.[2] Various cities have taken first steps to ease the *hukou* process; for instance, they have initiated programs to allow the

[1] Wu, Xiaogang, *The Household Registration System and Rural-Urban Educational Inequality in Contemporary China: Research report*, can be found at: http://www.psc.isr.umich.edu/pubs/pdf/rr11-735.pdf

[2] www.chinadaily.com.cn, retrieved on Mar. 27th, 2013; Chan, Kam Wing, Zhang, Li, *The Hukou System and Rural-Urban Migration in China: Processes and Changes*, can be found at http://www.upf.edu/materials/huma/central/historia/xinaXXI/lectures/Chan0.pdf

© Springer International Publishing Switzerland 2015

H.R. Randau, O. Medinskaya, *China Business 2.0*, Management for Professionals,
DOI 10.1007/978-3-319-07677-5_29

integration of rural migrant children in the education system. However, the measures are new and not yet sufficient.[3]

The *hukou* system in combination with the fact that rural farmers are not allowed to own and sell the land they work on (Chap. 17) makes rural farmers second class citizens. As China depends on further urbanization it will be forced to find ways to continue attracting rural people to the cities and integrating them into the urban regions. Urban housing is expensive and the fact that migrants have only limited access to urban welfare schemes is clearly a significant draw-back. As a consequence, the government will have to further liberalize the *hukou* system. New concepts such as a limited *hukou* in which new migrants to cities are offered partial access to pension and healthcare services for a limited time, or even an entire elimination of the *hukou* system are two possible options. Certainly *hukou* liberalization will be a complex task, as on one hand it requires further investment in the infrastructure for the related education and welfare services. On the other hand, it depends on ways of funding for local governments who are already under financial stress and whose expenses exceed their revenues (Chap. 25).

TIPS, OPPORTUNITIES and WARNINGS

Tip: Consider *hukou* in your recruiting strategy

Employers need to recognize that *hukou* is very important to employees and may greatly influence which jobs they will decide to take. In fact, receiving and maintaining *hukou* could be the determining factor whether or not a potential employee accepts a job offer.

[3] *Chinese Education Inequality To Be Reduced*, 06.09.2012, can be found at http://www.chinadaily.com.cn

Work Culture and Effective Management Style 30

China's work culture is still strongly influenced by traditional Confucian values, even though newer generations of Chinese employees are beginning to challenge these old standards.

In earlier days, organizations tended to be built on loyalty, or *guanxi* (Chap. 46), rather than merit. The leader would choose staff according to personal and professional connections—people who the leader knew would be loyal. This provided leaders security in their position and ensured that strong subordinates would not attempt to replace them. Many local companies still operate in this manner. The concept may have lost some of its dominance, but personal loyalty still holds great influence in company life and is often valued more highly than company loyalty. Because of this, Chinese companies face a great risk when key personnel leave, since their colleagues often follow suit due to *guanxi*.

In China, hierarchy and title are highly respected in the workplace. The management style tends toward the directive; instructions, opinions, and decisions are rarely questioned or criticized. Whether at a staff meeting or in public, employees will usually not disagree with the leader—this would cause a loss of face for all parties concerned. Often subordinates will not say "no" when given a task, even if it is impossible to accomplish. Given impossible tasks, they may provide an alibi or not even attempt the task, but say nothing in the hope that someone else takes the blame.

The hierarchical approach has helped Chinese companies to operate with speed and focus in an ever-changing environment. But the deference to authority it invokes, combined with Chinese education's emphasis on rote learning, have also strong disadvantages: it often leads to comparatively less creativity and personal initiative amongst employees. Silo mentality is pervasive and strong in Chinese organizations, with little sense of overall responsibility outside the scope of work.

Not surprisingly, Chinese employees are often less comfortable with matrix organizations which require reporting to multiple managers or supervisors. Chinese employees may also have difficulty dealing with high degrees of uncertainty, and

© Springer International Publishing Switzerland 2015

H.R. Randau, O. Medinskaya, *China Business 2.0*, Management for Professionals,
DOI 10.1007/978-3-319-07677-5_30

when faced with situations without explicit orders—where they may be unsure of what to do—they may post-pone decision making which slows the process.

China's companies and their employees tend to be rather flexible. Because of their experiences working in a rapidly changing environment, they are inclined to schedule meetings on short notice, respond directly to emails and phone calls, and implement decisions very quickly. While this flexibility certainly has big advantages, it can also be problematic, as it may prompt decisions without the appropriate analysis or organization.

In general, employees are motivated by rewards and recognition. They often focus on attaining financial success, security, and a positive perception in the public eye. A benefit of this is that—given the right incentives—Chinese employees have a progressive, competitive spirit. On the other hand, it is often only work that is visible is well-executed. Work that will not be rewarded with praise, merit, or money may be poorly executed, or even ignored. Sometimes competition can also become unhealthy as co-workers impede each other's productivity and jockey for authority in their positions. Even managers, having risen through the company hierarchy, may suffer from an "emperor of the office" complex: a focus on garnering praise and deflecting criticism rather than on growing the underlying business. The latter can have a trickledown effect, harming the atmosphere and attitude of all the manager's subordinates.

The following chart lists some typical behaviors and expectations that Chinese employees exhibit in their workplace, and how managers can use them to the business' larger success—without stepping on any cultural toes (Table 30.1).

Table 30.1 How to effectively manage Chinese employees

Chinese employees...		Effective managers...
Employees want clear instructions and guidance from superiors, as well as defined areas of authority and responsibility		Delegate tasks and projects clearly. Emphasize the group's responsibility for their aggregate results, rather than individual responsibility for component results. This discourages unhealthy competition and power struggles among employees
Employees value and influenced by personal connections and obligations (*guanxi*), so building a *guanxi* network is important		Try to build positive *guanxi* with employees by taking an interest in their personal lives and hobbies. Be sure to participate in and encourage company social events or sports teams. Always keep promises and return favors—this is the "currency" of *guanxi!*
Employees try to give others *face* and maintain their own *face* in professional interactions		Check on employees frequently—this gives them the opportunity to bring up problems and issues with projects in an way that maintains their *face*. Reward and recognize good performance publicly, and only give criticism privately (even then, be constructive!)
Employees give strong respect to hierarchy and titles Managers are obeyed and very rarely criticized		Act competent and professional at all times, trying to fit the image of a distant, but benevolent "*Confucian*" manger. Humbly accept but never seek praise. Don't succumb to "emperor of the office" mentality—encourage creativity and positive criticism when possible!

TIPS, OPPORTUNITIES and WARNINGS

Warning: High importance of informal communication

In China, the decision-making process requires much informal communication and deviates much from that in the west. In the west, even meetings of high ranking executives could include open discussion and exchange of ideas. In China, managers and stakeholders would have already exchanged ideas and arrived at a mutually beneficial agreement before the official meeting. The meeting marks the last step in such a process and is used to formalize a decision.

China also differs in that all high-ranking managers must be in agreement about key initiatives. This can lead to situations in which a whole project needs to be reconsidered if only one high-ranking manager is not convinced about an initiative or decision.

Tip: Avoid criticizing colleagues of subordinates publicly

This approach goes along with the concept of *face (mianzi)* and *connection (guanxi)*. Do not criticize staff, especially managers or supervisors, in front of their peers and never reprimand them when their subordinates are present. Such criticism has to be discussed in separate face-to-face meeting.

Tip: Fight the "silo" mentality

It is important to encourage cross-functional collaborations among a range of functional groups to break into the often present "silo" mentality of departments, functions or divisions. Get-togethers, workshops and team activities, along with a top-down managerial emphasis on the importance of cross-functional work, may be useful.

Tip: Reach out to Generation Y

It will be essential for companies to find ways to meet the younger generation's needs and to keep them motivated. This generation, which makes up nearly 50% of the country's workforce, is unlikely to tacitly accept outdated business practices and social structures.

INSIGHT: Nandani Lynton, CEIBS University

1) Working with China's Generation Y

Raised as only children burdened by the academic expectations and dreams of parents and grandparents, many Gen Ys suffer from unhealthy anxiety and perfectionism that can create self-doubt, performance anxiety, and, ultimately, procrastination.

Many managers find Gen Y members ambitious and demanding, hypersensitive, and almost allergic to criticism. They are puzzled by the amount of "emotion" Gen Y employees add to the workplace. Though they take for granted that hierarchy exists, Gen Ys do not comply with hierarchic rules in the way the previous generation—the generation of their managers—does. This creates friction between young staffers and supervisors.

Gen X middle managers tend to be less assertive, and may rarely voice opinions in meetings, yet they are now managing groups of young people with good English skills who are fully confident in speaking up and in interacting with foreigners. The young want to take initiative and share ideas but lack experience. Their immediate bosses at the middle level may thus feel squeezed, disrespected, and unable to deal with their young subordinates.

2) Attractive Messages for Generation Y

Message	Explanation
You will work with intelligent, creative colleagues	They long for good role models. When asked, Gen Ys often mention Apple (AAPL) CEO Steve Jobs, who is cool, creative, successful, and has a clear personal image.
You will be given meaningful challenges	Companies do well to share information and future strategies with Gen Ys. Brainstorming with these gifted staff members on projects or approaches can generate ideas that managers might never have thought of on their own. Being involved creates a sense of pride and a feeling that they are doing something important. The key is to give Gen Ys some influence.
You will achieve your personal goals.	Gen Ys are looking for positive career opportunities and ample chance for upward mobility. They are very individualistic and often more interested in their personal career prospects than any wider company goals.

You will be trained and will have a mentor	Gen Ys have grown up with grandparents, parents, and teachers all telling them what to do. They do not want to be told what to do and how to do it. But Gen Ys do have a strong desire to learn and receive training that will better qualify them. When managing Gen Ys, rather than using an authoritarian approach, focusing on guidance may be more effective. Instead of telling workers what to do, it is better to wait for the right time to drop by their desk and ask: "Have you asked yourself X? Perhaps you might have tried Y?"

Human Resource Challenges: Retention and Skills 31

Most managers run into two major problems in dealing with Chinese human resources: one is retaining staff and the other is improving employees' technical and managerial skill sets.

31.1 Retention

Much has been said about China's rapid employee turnover and its negative effects on productivity and quality. As in any high-growth emerging economy, labor continues to be in great demand. In particular, labor-intensive industries with a large number of low-paid workers saw high fluctuation rates. Young employees and migrant workers tended to be the ones who have been changing the most frequently.

Compensation was and will remain a fundamental retention factor. This is certainly not surprising, given the low salaries compared with others around the world, the hiking cost of living in urban areas, and the need to save money for child education or elderly support, due to a weak, if non-existing, social security net.

However, even for blue collar workers, a high compensation has not been the sole reason for staying with their employer. In recent years workers have begun to carefully evaluate whether the compensation and additional benefits, such as supplementary insurance schemes (health care, pension) and child education, have been worth the physical demands, work conditions, and the health and safety standards of their jobs. In addition, many employees have been seeking long-term contracts because of the restrictions in social welfare they are facing due to the Chinese household registration system (Chap. 29). According to our own experience, which is backed by the findings of several studies, the company's growth is

© Springer International Publishing Switzerland 2015

H.R. Randau, O. Medinskaya, *China Business 2.0*, Management for Professionals,
DOI 10.1007/978-3-319-07677-5_31

another highly important retention factor.[1] Growth is associated with the company's strength, (foreign) management commitment, job security, and last but not least, high premiums, as it often leads to overtime payments.

White collar workers, even more so than blue collar workers, seek competitive salary packages with multiple benefits, although they also value career development opportunities just as much. Highly-qualified Chinese employees look for lasting career opportunities and demand clear career tracks that will offer leadership opportunities and international exposure or global exchange programs. Being accustomed to rapid growth, they tend to leave slow-growing companies because they associate them with limited development opportunities. It remains difficult to manage this group's expectations, as they expect to quickly rise the corporate ladder. They look for frequent promotions, often at a much faster rate than is practiced in western countries.

31.2 Skills

In the past, foreign companies were mainly concerned with transferring technical know-how and implementing their corporate culture (e.g. in regards to quality and safety for their Chinese subsidies). Their strong efforts have paid off, as the workforce has made great progress internalizing these concepts, even though there is still plenty of room for further improvement.

In the future, it will not be enough to just implement western systems. As China's low-cost advantage diminishes over time, businesses will be pressured to look for ways to increase productivity. These companies moving up the value chain will additionally face the challenge of needing to manage increasingly complex value chains. This will demand new approaches and will require different skill sets to succeed. Accordingly, employers will increasingly seek employees with managerial qualifications and leadership skills.

Finding qualified candidates may prove to be challenging. Today, most Chinese managers display comparably weak leadership and execution skills. This is not surprising, as the current leadership generation grew up in a government-controlled hierarchical structure. This generation has adapted well to challenges brought on by the new economic environment. However, Chinese managers still have many limitations due to their inferior level of competence compared to those in western countries. Thus the quality of output fails to reach level of similar employees in mature markets.[2] This will undoubtedly change with the new generation—now in their 20s—that has been raised in a more liberalized, competitive environment.

[1] Michael Page (http://www.michaelpage.com.cn/websitepdf/ChinaEmployeeIntentionsReport201213_FINAL.pdf) (http://www.ddiworld.com/DDIWorld/media/trend-research/employee-retention-in-china-2007_fullreport_ddi.pdf).

[2] Mercer (http://www.mercer.com/articles/china-2012-business-leaders-top-talent-challenges-en), retrieved on Jan. 7th, 2014.

Some of these young candidates have had the opportunity to gain international experience, yet still the vast majority of these future managers have been brought up in an educational system that emphasizes learning by repetition rather than taking initiatives and managing complex tasks.

The current demand for highly-qualified employees with technical, sales, and managerial talents is likely to grow significantly faster than the supply of candidates. Given the serious shortage of skilled and experienced talent, businesses need to find solutions to address this problem. Employers will most likely be forced to set up their own training initiatives. Large multinationals could invest in in-house academies, although smaller corporations will probably have to join forces with similar businesses; in any case, additional skill-building initiatives will be unavoidable. Establishing close links to local colleges/universities is already a successful approach used by many foreign companies to help ensure that employees are learning the right skills.

Regarding the content, special emphasis must be given to develop managerial skills and leadership abilities, as well as to drive initiatives. For those businesses that decide to move up the value chain their increasingly complex business setups will require better internal collaboration. Overcoming departmental barriers, team building, and open communication should also be emphasized.

TIPS, OPPORTUNITIES and WARNINGS

Tip: Communicate your vision

Trust and loyalty are central elements of Chinese culture. Foreign companies are especially advised to clearly communicate their vision and strategy to all staff. Displaying their commitment to China (e.g. through investments and trainings) can be a crucial factor in keeping labor fluctuation rates at a reasonable level.

Tip: Set yourself apart from other employers

You must be sure that your current salaries and benefits remain competitive in the market. Employers need to provide an adequate value proposition through competitive base pays and benefits in order to retain employees.

Tip: Customize trainings to the Chinese culture

Chinese tend to sincerely believe that their culture and approach to doing business is unique in every aspect. Accordingly, trainings that do not encompass local context are not well received, if completely rejected. Based on our experiences, trainings based on local examples and taught by Chinese teachers are much more successful. Thus, taking simply advantage of global trainings is not advisable. Instead, training courses should at least be localized to a certain extent and reflect the Chinese culture.

Tip: Focus on practice-oriented learning

The Chinese often feel that classroom participation and certificates serve as proof of their competencies. Certainly this is not enough, especially in acquiring managerial or leadership skills. Employers need to respect their employees' efforts but also emphasize that theoretical knowledge needs to be linked to actual business practice. Establishing frequent real-life trainings might be an approach to link theory and practice.

Tip: Develop leadership skills of Chinese managers

The lack of leadership skills is a severe problem in China on all organizational levels. Especially on the shop floor, softer skills are sometimes missing, even if technical skills might be present. Employees tend to simply react to problems instead of looking for their root causes. Establishing formal meetings and teaching problem solving skills are a few approaches that may be successful.

INSIGHT: Hanno D. Wentzler and Bettina Schoen, Freudenberg Group

Attracting and retaining employees in China

The tremendous growth of the Chinese economy during the past years makes the fight for a loyal staff one of the biggest challenges for employers. A hot labor market combined with low birth rates and an aging population reduces the available talent pool. Companies heavily invest to attract top talents, but neglect to invest in onboarding and continuous people development resulting in unusually high turnover rates and, hence, ineffectiveness. Freudenberg believes that our associates are our core asset. Consequently, high focus is put on a solid recruiting process, training and leadership development, relating to our specific set of values – all in the context of the Chinese culture.

Know why one leaves

One key to solve the problem is to learn why people leave in the first place. Detailed reports regarding staff fluctuation, measured on a quarterly basis in all Freudenberg companies in China, combined with independent exit interviews ensure that top management has the transparency to evaluate the retention performance and enable swift reaction.

Retention Tools

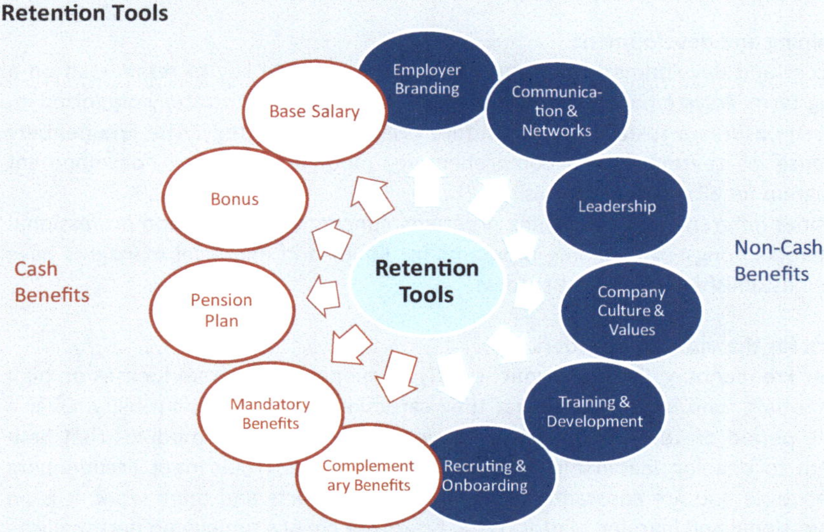

Strategies to retain employees

Traditional Chinese values compete with the highly dynamic and fast moving environment. Young Chinese have to cope with high requirements and expectations both from their employers and their families. Only an integrated strategy considering monetary and non-monetary aspects of retention can ensure an equivalent commitment in the future.

Compensation

Chinese employees pay high attention to their monthly take-home pay. A higher fixed part in early career stages and, later, an increasing variable part, paid performance-based bonuses, are common. Freudenberg tries to ensure competitive compensation and conducts frequent benchmarks. Complimentary benefits such as family health insurance or supplementary retirement benefits become more important and play an important role in the company's retention strategy.

Company culture

As a family owned company with a history of 165 years, Freudenberg has derived company specific "Values and Principles" from its successful past defining a consistent and firm basis for the daily working conduct and behavior. Increasing awareness for compliance and these principles is the objective of a series of compliance and integrity trainings for all top and midlevel leaders in Chinas. The high appreciation of the Chinese employees for these trainings documents the effectiveness of the approach.

Training and development

Career and development opportunities are the ultimate key to retain staff on a long-term. A systematic and individual career development strategy organized in-house ensures a sustainable and future oriented HR-strategy. The Freudenberg "House of Learning" is a comprehensive, modular training & development program for all employee levels.

Besides different generic training programs, functional trainings and professional networks, long-term training programs for junior and mid-level managers have been established with great success.

Care for the upcoming leaders

The "Freudenberg Talent Summit" (FCST) development program focuses on high potentials, who have proven that they can take on more responsibility. Over a time period of 18-24 month the participants pass different modules that help them to develop leadership skills and competencies. They meet Freudenberg executives and are constantly challenged with projects and team work. It is an educational and learning platform that offers the chance to develop personally as well as functionally and establishes a network among young professionals within the company that helps to meet and exchange on a regular basis, also strengthening the "family" feeling.

The Campus-Connection

A constant pipeline of young professionals is important to master future needs in a fast growing organization. Therefore, the close cooperation with top universities in China helps to identify and attract promising talent. University graduates have a chance for an internship or an international trainee program in Freudenberg. A necessary tool in an integrated approach, namely grow your own.

Employer branding

Employer branding plays a crucial role. Freudenberg has established a systematic communication strategy that emphasizes what the company stands for. Internal communication tools help the employees to understand the company's long-term vision, strategies, achievements and financial performance. Identification with Freudenberg and commitment to the company are measurable effects. Strong external communication through regular press conferences and executive media interviews help to attract employees from outside and nourishes the staffs' pride being part of the "family".

Conclusion

The toolkit to increase employee satisfaction provides a lot: the right hiring decision, competitive pay, a caring boss who nourishes his talent with new challenges, highly professional training and learning opportunities and a systematic career development program. A vivid company culture and a solid reliable leadership behavior, professional networking and a transparent communication culture add to that and offer opportunities to significantly increase staff loyalty.

Suggestions for Further Reading

China International Intellectech Corporation	www.ciicbj.com/english/
Foreign Enterprise Service Corporation (FESCO)	www.fesco.com.cn
Hays	www.hays.cn
Mercer Human Resource Consulting	www.mercer.com
Michael Page International	www.michaelpage.com

32 Playing by the Rules: Employment Regulations

The Chinese labor market remains highly inflexible due to complex employment legislation and constraints in the ability of inward migrants to fill talent gaps (hukou system).[1]

The key framework is the PRC Labor Law that was introduced 1995 and is applicable to all employment relationships in China (for details on general working conditions see table below). Recently, the government has enacted several laws to better protect the labor force and has adopted clear regulations on working hours, minimum wages, holidays, and social security contributions, which apply to local and Foreign Invested Enterprises alike.

In practice this major legislation is supplemented by many local regulations, which provide detailed explanations and guidance on China's Labor Law. Thus, when dealing with employment issues in China foreign companies may need to refer to local regulations in addition to the Labor Law.

32.1 Recruitment

China's hiring regulations differ from other countries in several ways. Written contracts, for instance, require the specification of a resident ID and labor protection information, which is dictated by a citizen's *hukou* (Chap. 18).

Joint Ventures and WFOEs can employ staff from the local workforce directly while ROs are required to hire staff through an authorized labor agency such as the Foreign Enterprise Service Corporation (FESCO) or the China International Intellectech Corporation (CIIC). ROs must also establish a contractual relationship with the labor agency and pay the required service fee.

[1] Hays rate China's inflexibility at >8 on scale from 0 to 10 with 10 representing the highest amount of inflexibility. See *The Hays Global Skills set 2012*, can be found at: www.hays.com

© Springer International Publishing Switzerland 2015

H.R. Randau, O. Medinskaya, *China Business 2.0*, Management for Professionals,
DOI 10.1007/978-3-319-07677-5_32

Foreign firms will often bring non-Chinese employees to their Chinese work sites. For this practice, there are several kinds of business visas which differ by business purpose, period of stay, and skills (seniority-level). Hiring foreign employees to work in China normally requires a "Z" or "R" visa—an employment permit and residency certificate. Companies also must demonstrate that the special abilities or experience of the potential foreign employee are not available within the Chinese workforce. Importantly, the foreign employee must have a clean criminal record.

32.2 Labor Agreements

Employment in China is divided into full-time and part-time employment (no more than 4 h per day and 24 h per week). Employment relationships can be fixed term, open-ended, or project-based.

Limited employment contracts on a full-time basis are the dominant form of employment in China. All full-time labor contracts must be in writing and completed within 1 month of employment. The labor contract may contain a probationary period, the length of which depends on the length of the contract. Since China lacks an At-Will Employment Policy, laying-off employees can be a rather involved process. For more details, see Table 32.1.

32.3 Wages, Benefits and Social Security

Wages are based on either time or piecework but cannot be less than the minimum wage standard. The minimum wage is promulgated on provincial level and adjusted annually.

China has reduced regular working time to 40 h per week and has introduced clear regulations on overtime payment.

The law requires that upon obtaining a business license, a company must establish related Social Security Accounts. Social security contributions are calculated as a percentage of base salary, and can vary from 20 % up to 44 % (Figs. 32.1 and 32.2).

Table 32.1 Major HR regulations in China

Working hours
• 40 h per week (5 days with 8 h)
Overtime regulations
• Max overtime is 36 h per month. Work > 8 h limited by law and must be paid at 150 % of normal rate. Work on 6th and 7th day in the week must be paid 200 % of the contract rate. Work on Chinese National Holidays or unused paid annual vacations: 300 % of the base rate. There are 11 statutory public holidays per annum (→Chinese Festivals)
Special allowances
• For the manufacturing industry: Mandatory high temperature allowance for (a) employees who work outdoors under high temperature (35° centigrade or higher) and (b) employees who work indoors where the work place temperature cannot be lowered to below 33° centigrade
Minimum wage
• Determined by the specific regulations of each province. Wages may vary depending on the industry and the location within the province • Minimum wage is defined as salary excluding mandatory social insurance, housing fund and overtime payment
Social security
• Social security accounts include pensions, basic medical, unemployment, maternity and work-related injury insurance
Paid annual vacations
• Normally 5–20 days annual leave, determined according to the employee's position and years of service • Generally, the minimums are as follows: 1 to 10 years–5 days; 10 to 20 years–10 days; >20 years–15 days
Probation period
• The maximum probation period is based on the term of the contract but probation salaries cannot be less than 80 % of the employee's future contractual salary • Probation periods according to contract length: <3 months—no probation period applicable; 3 months to 1 year—max. 1 month; 1 to 3 years—2 months, >3 years—up to 6 months
Age requirement
• Males must be between 18 and 60 years of age • Females must be 18–55
Termination of employment
• A labor contract may be terminated if the employee is found incapable of performing during the probation period, violates rules in a significant way, commits serious dereliction of duty or practices graft, becomes criminally convicted, or establishes employment with another company which materially affects the completion of tasks with the employer • The employee may also terminate a contract by giving the employer a 30-day written prior written notice • Unlike practices in many other countries, "employment at will" is not permitted in China. In the United States, for instance, the majority of states have adopted "at-will" employment, whereby employers are given a lot of power over which employees to keep. In China, however, Article 38 of the PRC Labor Contract Law makes an employer's right to unilaterally end a labor contract rather limited • Enterprises may need to give a statutory termination notice and provide required severance payment. By law, the severance payment is calculated based on the actual service year and the salary level of the staff • Termination is prohibited if an employee suffers from work-related injuries and is under medical observation, or if it can be proven that the employee has lost ability to work due to

(continued)

Table 32.1 (continued)

occupational hazards or diseases. To ensure the diagnosis of such injuries, an exit health check-up for those exposed to occupational hazards is mandatory. Employers may not terminate contracts during medical treatment periods, pregnancy, confinement or nursing periods • A special non-termination rule applies for employees that have worked over 15 consecutive years for one employer and are less than 5 years away from retirement
Severance and compensation after termination by fixed-term contracts
• Severance pay should equal the employee's monthly salary multiplied by the employee's number of years of service. However, the monthly salary used in this calculation may not exceed three times the average salary in the local municipality. Severance packages are not compulsory in China, unless stipulated in the employee's contract
Noncompetition agreement
• Such an agreement should be limited to senior management and other employees with access to critical trade secrets • Non-competition periods can last a maximum of 2 years. During this period a person is not allowed to work for a competing employer, establish their own similar business, or produce similar products on their own • The restriction must be limited to a reasonable geographic area • After the termination of the employment contract, the employer must pay the employee monthly compensation according to the non-competition agreement for the length of the competition restriction

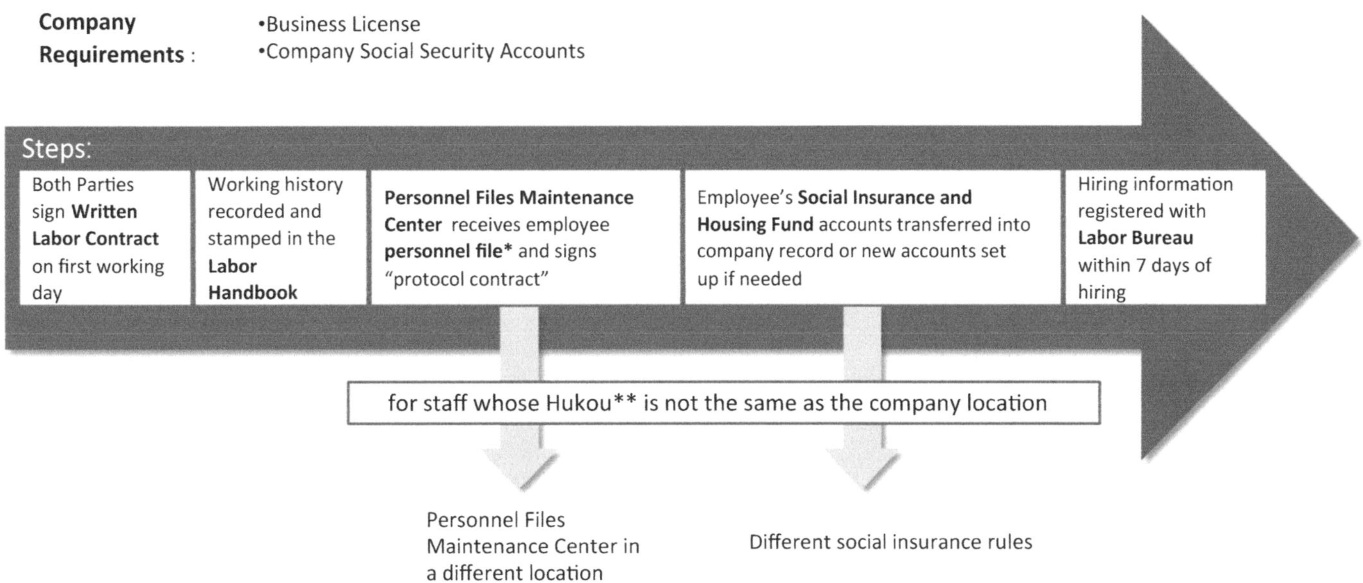

*A personnel file is a document each Chinese possesses as a record of their work experiences, education, criminal records, and other related details. The government uses these files to oversee the movement of individuals

**Designated residence of employee (chap. 18)

Fig. 32.1 Hiring process for Chinese employees

TIPS, OPPORTUNITIES and WARNINGS

Tip: Stay in touch with local labor authorities is important

It is essential to be proactive regarding broad, unspecific, and ambiguous human-resource regulations. Because these regulations are imprecise, they can be interpreted in many ways. Thus, most labor disputes end up in mediation courts. Therefore, close contact with local authorities is important, as it will save you a lot of trouble in the end.

Warning: One playground, two sets of rules

Foreign companies generally face higher expectations in terms of wages and compliance with regulations. Violations by foreign companies tend to result in comparably higher penalties, as western companies are believed to be financially well-off and thus able to pay the fines.

INSIGHT: Bryant J. Eggett, Mercer Consulting

Legal Human Resource Regulations

Still a developing system

The Chinese legal system has made great strides in the last decade but is still developing. Executives need to be aware that contracts do not have the same status that they do in western courts, and companies have little recourse in the event of unfavorable actions by powerful local officials or other actors.

Labor disputes often result in arbitration

Dispute resolution through legal channels remains difficult. The law is written to favor employees. Most labor related cases are forwarded to arbitration courts and will eventually lead to "harmonious" agreements of any kind. Foreign companies need to be aware that courts often hold them to extremely high standards of evidence to win cases in court.

Strong Employee Protection

Employees are generally better protected when compared to some western countries (e.g. USA): they are not subject to "at-will" firing, and an employee can unilaterally end an employment contract giving 30 days' notice. Additionally, China has implemented strong disability protection clauses.

Western companies need to be compliant

As in other fields, western companies tend to be held responsible to be strictly compliant with regulations. Sometimes even small violations can result in penalties and usually get large media attention with potentially devastating results for the company's reputation.

Suggestions for Further Reading

Ministry of Human Resources and	www.mohrss.gov.cn

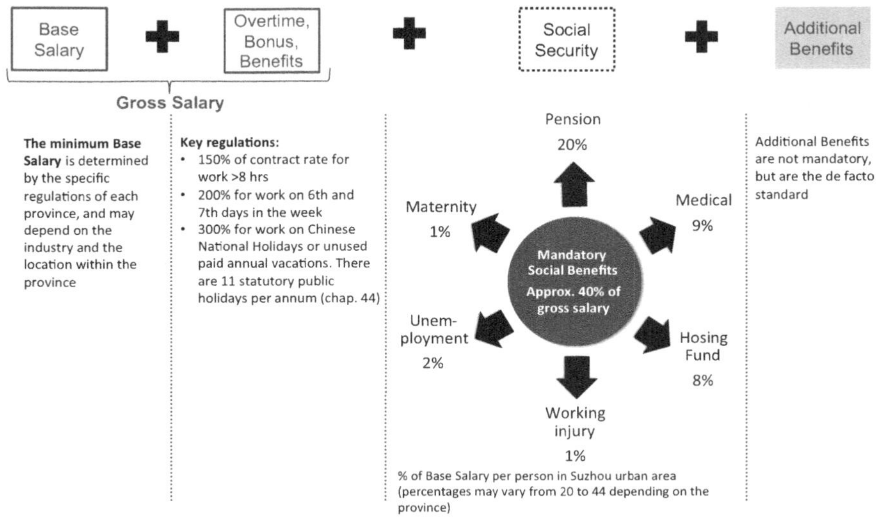

Fig. 32.2 Salary calculation

33 The Education System: The Big Picture

Education holds great importance in China, opening the door to promising professional careers, wealth, and financial security for the whole family. The Chinese strongly believe that a school or university with a better reputation gives a better education and assures a good future. Accordingly, Chinese are willing to invest a huge part of their income on their children's education.

The education system was nearly destroyed by the negative impacts of the cultural revolution. In recent years China has made rapid progress in improving the system once again. Initially built around "key" schools and universities for a small elite (a concept that still exists today on a small scale), the leadership has implemented numerous reforms to resolve the problems of disparity and inequality in education. These initiatives were geared towards raising the standard of education across the country and included school ratings to achieve minimum standards, increased public funds for rural schools, and systematic teacher transfers (urban teachers sent to rural areas and vice versa).

However, the system still emphasizes repetitive learning rather than deep understanding and problem-solving skills. Thus, it has strong limitations in producing school graduates with creative, critical or transformative thinking skills. As a nation dedicated to moving up the value chain, China will face the pressure to make further significant reforms to its education system in the future.

33.1 School Education

The Chinese education system is structured similarly to western countries. Education starts at the age of three when children enter preschool, and formal education begins at the age of 6.

As the Compulsory Education Law stipulates, each child must have a minimum of 9 years of formal education: 6 years in primary school and another 3 years in junior secondary level. Those first 9 years are generally free but linked (as the acceptance to preschool) to the *hukou* (Chap. 29) and a certificate of property

© Springer International Publishing Switzerland 2015
H.R. Randau, O. Medinskaya, *China Business 2.0*, Management for Professionals,
DOI 10.1007/978-3-319-07677-5_33

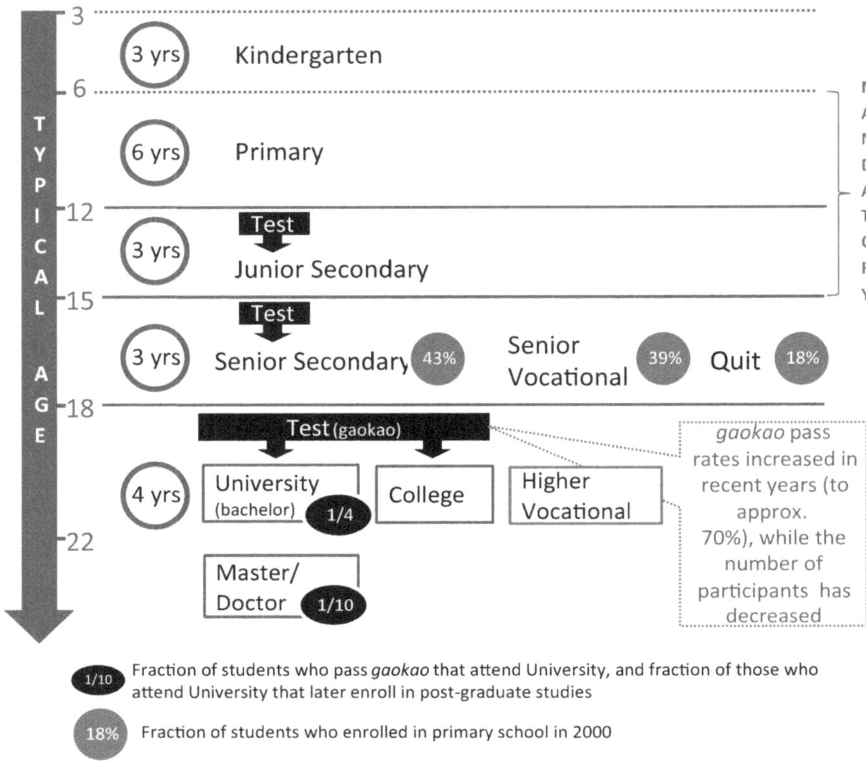

Fig. 33.1 Chinese education system. *Source*: China Statistical Yearbook 2013

ownership from the parents. Thus, the compulsory education has been a big positive move of the last decade. The fact that schools are still charging fees to poor rural children whose parents have no *hukou* remains a serious problem which perpetuates inequalities. Only 10 %[1] of migrant children are currently completing junior high school which is a major problem, if China seriously intends to upgrade the workforce.

Any student wishing to continue education may attend vocational school or try to qualify for senior secondary school by passing the appropriate entrance examination. The test results determine which school, good or bad, they will attend. Only 30–50 % pass the exam but children with lower scores can still be accepted if they pay enough money.

In any case, Senior Secondary education is not free. The annual fee is several thousand Yuan in public schools and much more in private schools. The first 2 years are usually material intensive while the last year often repeats and enforces previous content in preparation for the National Education Entrance Examination (*gaokao*)—the standardized university entrance exam (Fig. 33.1).

[1] Green, Stephen, China- Dreaming of economic reform in 2013, Standard Chartered Global Research, 2013.

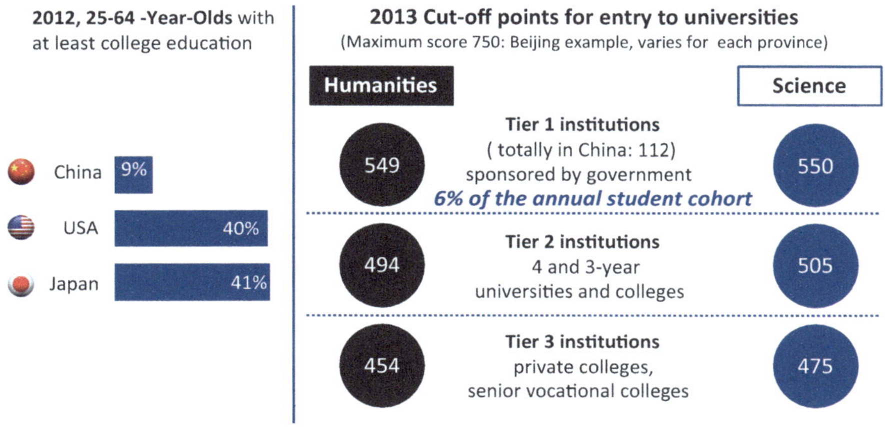

Fig. 33.2 Admission scores by Post-Secondary Institution. *Source*: http://gaokao.eol.cn, http://edu.people.com.cn

Since grades in secondary school do not influence university admission, students are pressured to achieve high *gaokao* scores. Consequently, this 3-day-examination is a major event in the students' and families' lives.

Scheduled nationally in early June, *gaokao* contents vary from one province to another. Students must choose a university and a major before taking the exam, and the exam score then determines whether the student is admitted. If the student's score is too low for the selected major, the university may offer admission in a different one. If the potential student does not agree with the adjusted major he or she will have to change schools, but since the school's name is more highly valued than the major, few choose this option (Fig. 33.2).

33.2 Higher Education

Almost all Chinese universities are publicly owned and run by provincial or central governments. There are a few private undergraduate colleges, mostly engineering schools, the vast majority of which are not entitled to give bachelor degrees. The reputation of the university holds highest importance to a successful career. A reputed university name makes way for a successful career path regardless of major, as these graduates, who have defeated millions of competitors to be accepted there, are always in high demand. All colleges charge tuition that is usually around 6,000 Yuan, but varies by school, city, and major. Though private colleges usually have higher fees (often at least twice as much), they tend to have worse reputations (Wang 2011).

Chinese leadership is aware that it must not only increase the number of Chinese university graduates but also improve the quality of their education in order to fulfill its growth and innovation objectives.

Lately the number of Chinese students abroad has risen significantly and those who are fortunate enough are often willing to send their children abroad. This gives children careers that do not solely depend on their *gaokao* score. Students who return from abroad as well-trained professionals are the most sought after by employers. The most popular country of study is the US, followed by Australia, Japan, Britain, South Korea, Canada and Singapore.

33.3 Learning and Pressure on Children

Education in China still follows traditional Confucian values: students are expected to learn from experienced teachers by displaying obedience and discipline and knowledge is acquired through repetition rather than gradual understanding of the material. Only after students have mastered material by rote are they allowed creative or autonomous input into their education.

Chinese are known throughout the world as dedicated and high-performing students, but they have little choice because the one child policy has prompted families to focus all their ambitions on the only child. Accordingly, pressure on children is very high, often starting as early as kindergarten when teachers coach the children for entrance examinations to a primary school. The dictates of examinations have left students with little relatively little room to enjoy personal preferences and they are usually forced by their parents to spend most of their limited free time attending music classes, foreign language courses, or other curricula designed by their parents.

TIPS, OPPORTUNITIES, and WARNINGS

Warning: Limited equivalences of titles and quality of education

Potential employers must be aware that many graduates hold titles which are not anywhere close to being equivalent to similar degrees in western countries.

Warning: Students lack practical experience

Students are usually well-trained in following instructions and applying established practices, but have trouble developing new ideas and solutions. They may also lack practical work experience and are often immature compared to western students. Additional training may be necessary to get these graduates used to the work environment in western companies.

Warning: Top students can be demanding and difficult to integrate

Companies seeking top-university graduates should consider that such students may be tough to integrate and retain. Since they are able to find many job alternatives in the market, they not only demand a higher salary, but often also expect special training, higher status, exposure to the top management, and quick promotions.

The overall university ranking 2013 (from Netbig, an Internet site focused on higher education) is based upon indices in four categories including academic quality, student quality, teaching resources and research funding (Table 33.1).

Table 33.1 Top 30 Chinese universities

1	Tsinghua University	16	Wuhan University
2	Peking University	17	Huazhong University of Science and Technology
3	Zhejiang University	18	Tianjin University
4	University of Science and Technology of China	19	Beijing Normal University
5	Nanjing University	20	Jilin University
6	Fudan University	21	China Agricultural University
7	Shanghai Jiaotong University	22	Northwestern Polytechnical University
8	Harbin Institute of Technology	23	Central South University
9	Renmin University	24	Dalian University of Technology
10	Beijing University of Aeronautics and Astronautics	25	Southeast University
11	Nankai University	26	Shandong University
12	Sichuan University	27	East China Normal University
13	Xi'an Jiaotong University	28	Beijing Institute of Technology
14	Sun Yat-sen University	29	Tongji University
15	Xiamen University	30	Beijing University of Science and Technology

Suggestions for Further Reading

Ministry of of the People's Republic of China	www.moe.gov.cn

Reference

Wang, L. (2011). Social exclusion and inequality in higher education in China: A capability perspective. *International Journal of Educational Development, 31*(3), 277–286.

34 Chops: The Chinese Form of Signature

In China the colloquial name "chop" refers to the stamps and seals used in lieu of signatures to legally authorize documentation. A chop represents a legal organization, entity or natural person. The Company Chop is most important as it is required before any legal entity can conduct business activities. The company chop must be approved by the local Public Security Bureau (PSB) and is required on all official business documents as it is legally binding.

It is common that entities create various chops, each being used for different purposes, with only limited scope and power. These additional chops are not mandatory but provide company departments with the ability to serve their specific business requirements. The most common types of additional chops are:

- The Legal Representative Chop, which represents the signature (i.e. the authority) of the entity's designated legal representative and is filed with the Administration of Industry and Commerce. In combination with the Company Chop, it is required for numerous legal and official documents including applications for business licenses and tax certificates
- The Legal Finance Chop is used for financial transactions such as cash withdrawals, wire transfers, and changes to account information
- The Contract Chop is only used in place of or together with the Company Chop to validate binding contractual agreements
- The Human Resource Chop is used for signing labor contracts with employees, authenticating employment verification letters, and registering employees with government bodies and issuing internal memos

© Springer International Publishing Switzerland 2015

H.R. Randau, O. Medinskaya, *China Business 2.0*, Management for Professionals,
DOI 10.1007/978-3-319-07677-5_34

TIPS, OPPORTUNITIES, and WARNINGS

Warning: Monitor the use of the Company Chop closely

The possession of Chops should be strictly controlled, especially the Company Chop, as it is legally binding for the entire company, providing the possessor the authority to conduct business activities on behalf of the entity.

Negotiation: How to Make Deals in China 35

Negotiating in China requires an approach different from many countries in the West. Flexibility may be preferred and business interactions may be treated more as mutual bonds, even with elements of friendship, where exchanges occur as the need arises.

The negotiation process can be time-consuming, and before committing the time to establishing a business relationship, it is advisable to thoroughly investigate the background and reliability of the business and of key individuals. It may be best to examine, for instance, their quality of corporate governance, the value of their products, and their current financial status.

Once it has been decided to move ahead and try to create a contract with a business, the first step is to build trust. This usually takes several rounds of back-and-forth communication—through meetings or dinner outings—and ideally results in the establishment of *guanxi* (Chap. 46). With this trust focus in mind, the Chinese remain opportunistic—often seeking the "trusted" partner who offers the nicest deal. So while significant time may need to be invested before serious business talks can take place, contract terms will also require a considerable amount of discussion.

To determine if the negotiating party is really interested in doing business, sending out a contract may be the best test. If interested, they will generally reply promptly—within a 1–2 week period. If the reply is not prompt, the party may not be interested, and if a deal is still sought, it is best to visit frequently to convince them that this deal would be in their best interest.

Term bargaining takes place throughout the entire negotiation process: even as trust is being built, term bargaining may already begin. Though closing a deal is difficult without *guanxi*, often a monetary anchor is set as initial quotes are being discussed during the first interactions. If there is a contract term or price which cannot be agreed upon within a reasonable time period, it is best to state as much in order to allow the negotiations to move forward. But when offering terms it is important to know what can be reasonably asked: the agreed price will generally be market driven, and one can find target prices through fairs and exhibitions, speaking

© Springer International Publishing Switzerland 2015

H.R. Randau, O. Medinskaya, *China Business 2.0*, Management for Professionals,
DOI 10.1007/978-3-319-07677-5_35

with competitors, checking Internet prices, visiting manufacturer's websites, and simply asking directly.

Typically, in China negotiation takes place by teams rather than as individuals. Usually one member of the Chinese negotiating group will be the key decision maker (often the most senior team member). Identification of this group member, as well as other players who might influence this person's decision, is essential. A team can achieve best negotiation results if it is patient in the decision making progress. The best means in gaining leverage in China is the attitude of indifference, rather than excitement or negative emotion.

TIPS, OPPORTUNITIES, and WARNINGS

Tip: Be patient

If during the negotiation process you are told something that seems a little strange or incorrect, it is best not to call this out. It is always important to stay calm regardless of true feelings or emotions in order to save face. The best strategy may be to pretend to believe what you have been told and do your own follow-up research afterwards. Then, if there are outstanding issues, it is best to talk them over during a one-to-one meeting with someone of the negotiating party of similar rank.

As mentioned, negotiation usually takes place in a team; it may be best to assign certain roles among team members. Having good cop – bad cop roles (the Chinese also often refer to the "white" and "black" face) can be especially effective and ties in well with the Chinese concept of harmony. The bad cop represents the yin, or black face, and should act doubtful and convey a negative attitude, while the good cop, the yang or white face, should balance out the bad cop with a more trusting and positive approach. Together, a harmony is created which, when properly executed, can help achieve the desired business goals and make for smooth negotiations.

INSIGHT: Joerg Wuttke, BASF China
President of the European Union Chamber of Commerce, China

Cultural Differences in Negotiations

Working with people from different cultures challenges one's ability to balance potentially conflicting ideas about how the world works (world view), about getting things done (practice), and about what is important (values). Each individual has opinions on these issues that are fundamental to the way he or she thinks. When moving within one's own culture, everyone shares the same mindset and it is therefore considered entirely natural. Only those individuals faced with strikingly different views in culturally diverse settings are forced to become aware of their own unquestioned assumptions about the world.

Negotiations are an arena in which cultural differences become quickly visible. One essential difference between Chinese and western approaches to negotiations is their differing views on the importance of legal processes. While Westerners stress the legalistic aspects of negotiations and consider the signed written contract an end-product and binding agreement, Chinese emphasize the strength of ethical and moral principles, and consider a contract simply a flexible part of an ongoing relationship. While it is advisable to join the Chinese in relationship building and seeking general agreement on large issues - and to use that positive atmosphere to advantage - Westerners have found they abandon the fine print at their peril. When disagreement arises, the Chinese have learned to be equally skilled at demanding fulfillment of a legal contract.

The negotiation process also illustrates basic differences in communication and social patterns. While Chinese typically spend time early on developing a relationship and discovering common interests, Northern Europeans and Americans are known for wanting to jump into business negotiations without "wasting time". The Chinese and Asian tendency to communicate important information in an indirect manner and to be evasive about difficulties often leads to severe misunderstandings with these same Westerners who both ask and answer even unpleasant questions with blunt honesty. The real difficulty arises when these communication styles lead to a lack of trust, with the Westerners viewing Chinese politeness as dishonesty, and the Chinese viewing western directness as insulting and suspicious. One can learn to communicate across styles; in conflict situations when adrenaline levels rise, however it takes patience and self-discipline not to fall into old habits.

Part IV

The Chinese Way

Confucius said, “The nature of men is always the same; it is their habits that separate them.” Understanding China’s unique socio-cultural environment and respecting its business etiquette are essential prerequisites for business success in China.

This part describes the primary influences shaping the Chinese society, discusses the political and administrative structure, and familiarizes you with basic social concepts, such as *mianzi* and *guanxi*. Wherever necessary, it gives you hands-on advice on how to conduct yourself in business settings with special emphasis on where Chinese and western values and customs deviate greatly from one another.

36 China and the West

Chinese civilization dates back more than 3,500 years but its cultural pillars emerged during the 300 years after the time of Confucius (500 B.C.).

36.1 The First Emperor

China's unification was led by the ruler of the *Qin,* whose kingdom emerged the strongest of seven warring states in around 221 B.C. After subjugating the other kingdoms, he declared himself first emperor of China (*Shi Huang Di*). Even though the *Qin* dynasty ended soon after his death, a unified China under imperial rule lasted for over 2,000 years. The first emperor is universally portrayed as a cruel ruler but his many accomplishments included standardized systems of writing, law, currency, and weights and measures. He established a central government, developed a national road system, expanded the Chinese empire, built a capital in Chang'an (modern day Xi'an) and undertook gigantic building projects, including the first version of the Great Wall, and the mausoleum of Terracotta Army soldiers.

36.2 Imperial China

Many different dynasties followed the *Qin,* some of which were conquest Dynasties founded by non-Han people like the Mongols (Yuán dynasty) and the *Manchu* (Qing dynasty). In the late fifteenth century the construction of the great wall as it is known today began, which accelerated China's strong isolationist politics. Even though foreign countries, through a combination of warfare and diplomacy, often sought power, influence, and greater trade in the region, isolationism prevailed until the mid-nineteenth century when China lost the First Opium War (1839–1842) to

© Springer International Publishing Switzerland 2015

H.R. Randau, O. Medinskaya, *China Business 2.0*, Management for Professionals,
DOI 10.1007/978-3-319-07677-5_36

the British. In the decades following the Opium Wars, further military defeats, economic hardship, and poverty continuously weakened the authority of the Qing dynasty and finally brought an end to imperial rule after a revolutionary military uprising in 1911.

36.3 Modern China

Following the uprising, the provisional government of the Republic of China was formed in Nanjing in March 1912 with Sun Yat-sen of the *Kuomintang*, or *Nationalist Party* (KMT), as president. But his attempt to organize a new democratic government failed and China drifted into the warlord era where much of the country was ruled by competing provincial military leaders.

In the 1920s Sun Yat-sen established a revolutionary base in South China and set out to unite the fragmented nation. After his death one of his followers, Chiang Kai-shek, gained control of KMT and succeeded in bringing most of South and Central China under his rule by military campaign.

Meanwhile, a new political faction called Communist Party of China (CPC) formed in 1921 opposing the KMT. Soon the two forces were involved in a Chinese Civil War which continued even after various parts of the country fell under Japanese occupation in 1931. Chased by *Kuomintang* armies, the CPC retreated through one of China's most difficult terrains to Shaanxi in the Northwest, an escape known as "the Long March". During the Long March the communists reorganized under a new leader, Mao Zedong. Even though the two parties formed a united front to oppose the Japanese during the Sino-Japanese War (1937–1945, which became part of World War II), the civil war resumed following Japan's defeat. The conflict finally ended in 1949 after the CPC had occupied most of the country. On October 1, 1949, Mao Zedong established the People's Republic of China (PRC) and much of the KMT (leadership, troops and a large number of their supporters) escaped to Taiwan.

36.4 The People's Republic of China

After China regained its independence Mao Zedong began to implement his vision of a socialist society. He drove this transformation largely through ideological movements, especially "The Great Leap Forward" and "The Cultural Revolution". "The Great Leap Forward" (1958–1961) was an economic growth program originally intended to increase the pace of industrialization. Unfortunately, this project, which involved a process called collectivization (a new agricultural technique whereby peasants were forced to work on massive, joint infrastructure projects instead of private food production), proved counterproductive: instead of increasing production, grain yields fell sharply. Combined with a subsequent drought, the program resulted in the largest man-made famine in human history (with over 30 million deaths).

Since Mao was held responsible for this failure, more pragmatic leaders arose and the nation found itself in a turbulent struggle between the two party fractions. In 1966 Mao, still chairman of the CPC, proved his power by launching the "Cultural Revolution" program, a campaign intended to identify liberal elements of society. He mobilized youths (known as the Red Guards) to investigate all levels of society in an effort to eliminate potential opponents. The result was a period of social chaos, great fear and suspicion, with millions being persecuted and imprisoned, and young intellectuals being "re-educated" through hard manual labor.

36.5 The New China

The death of Mao Zedong in 1976 marked the end of the Cultural Revolution. After a short struggle, the pragmatic wing of the CPC asserted its power against Mao's successor Hua Guofeng, and economic development soon became the priority. Lead by the new leader Deng Xiaoping, the government instituted the first free market economic reforms in 1978. These first reforms were almost instantly successful but they met a significant setback in 1989 after pro-democracy student demonstrations in Beijing's Tiananmen Square were viciously suppressed by the army. Deng supported the use of military weapons to end the protests as he was determined to maintain the party's monopoly on power. But after the event, conservative forces within the party gained momentum and forced him to formally retire from office. The party leadership was seriously divided into reformist and formalist factions and for some time it remained highly uncertain whether the reform process would be continued. Though he was politically weakened, Deng managed to rescue his economic reform from the conservative backlash. His famous southern tour of China in the spring of 1992 marked a visible step towards further reform. Initially ignored by national media, his visits of SEZ's (Special Economic Zones) accompanied by speeches emphasizing the need to continue reforms gained the support of much of the populace and laid the future path toward economic openness.

The transition of power following Deng Xiaoping's death (1997) to Jiang Zemin and Hu Jintao brought no major changes. The country continued to liberalize the economy while maintaining government control in key industries and avoiding significant political reforms.

36.6 The Attitude Towards the West

To this day, perhaps as a result of past oppression, many Chinese are wary of foreign influence, especially concerning the Japanese. This feeling was brought to a head recently in several territorial disputes.

China's apprehensive attitude towards foreign nations began taking shape in the mid-nineteenth century when the West was entering its age of imperialism and western countries were increasingly interested in gaining access to China and its markets. At the height of their imperial power, the British began selling opium in place of silver to China in order to fund their tea trade. Although China declared the drug illegal, the British-Chinese opium market flourished. Chinese addiction rates rose drastically and the two countries were thrown into the Opium Wars, from which the mightier Britain emerged victorious.

During British occupation, the Chinese opened ports to foreign trade, paid reparations, ceded or leased territories (such as Hong Kong to Great Britain and Macau to Portugal), and allowed foreign missionaries and embassies within the mainland. Other western nations managed to enforce similar treaties and even set up consular authorities (mainly in the port cities) reflecting their own judicial systems.

The unequal treaties imposed by foreign nations were a great insult to the Chinese. Popular sentiment resisted foreign influences and lead to continuous civil unrest and violent revolts. Best known is the infamous Boxer Uprising (1899–1901), when Chinese peasants began attacking foreign railroads, embassies, and missions. However, the most humiliating defeating for the Chinese was Japan's victory in the First Sino-Japanese War (1894–1895). As a result, the regional dominance in East Asia shifted from China to Japan and led to a decades-long Japanese imperialist policy aiming to dominate China politically and militarily.

This period of military defeats weakened the Qing dynasty's rule and many Chinese people lost faith in the current government and saw the need to modernize. This movement materialized in the Revolution of 1911, which brought an end to imperial rule in China. Even in the new republic, western powers continued their business in extraterritorial zones while Japan grew to become China's arch-enemy. Japan focused on the region of northeast China (Manchuria) in order to secure its vast raw material reserves. In 1932 the Japanese established the puppet state of Manchukuo, with China's last *Qing* emperor installed as the nominal regent and emperor. WWII broke out shortly after Japan began their conquest for the rest of China in the Second Sino-Japanese War (1937–1945). The Chinese lost nearly every battle, and Japanese occupation in China only ended when Japan was defeat by the allied forces (Fig. 36.1).

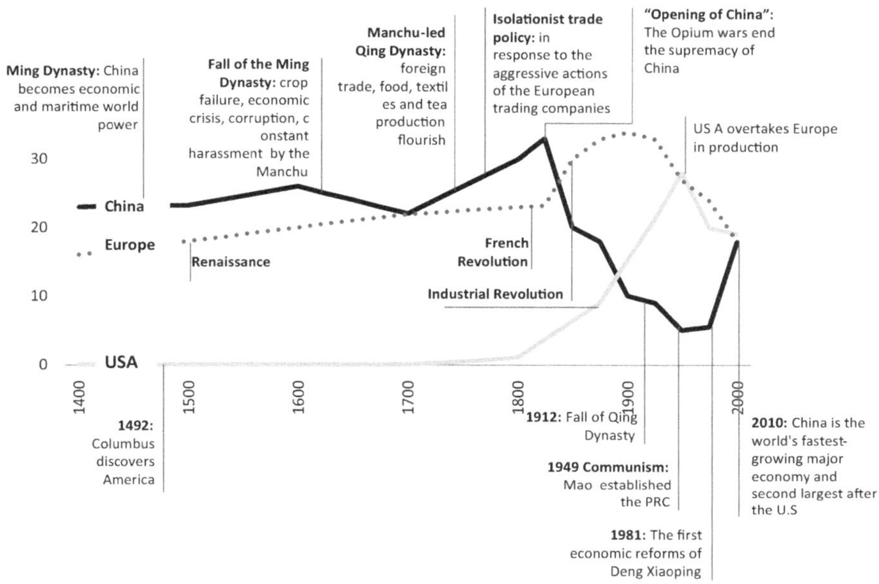

Fig. 36.1 Recent history timeline. *Source*: Used with kind permission from McKinsey & Company

Suggestions for Further Reading

Bickers, R. (2011). *The scramble for China: Foreign devils in the Qing Empire, 1832–1914*. London: Allen Lane.

Chang, J., & Jon, H. (2005). *Mao: The unknown story*. London: Jonathan Cape.

Fenby, J. (2008). *The fall and rise of a great power, 1850–2008*. London: Allen Lane.

Jacques, M. (2012). *When China rules the world: The end of the Western world and the birth of a new global order*. London: Penguin Books.

Portal, J. (Ed.). (2007). *The first emperor: China's terracotta army*. London: British Museum Press.

37 Administrative Structure and Ethnic Groups

37.1 Administrative Structure

The People's Republic of China (PRC) is divided under the Central Government into 22 provinces, 5 autonomous regions, and 4 direct-controlled municipalities. China also has two largely independent, self-governing Special Administrative Regions (SARs), Hong Kong and Macau. Even though the PRC claims Taiwan (Republic of China, ROC) as its 23rd province, Taiwan is actually a self-governing democracy that has never recognized the claim.

Provinces have their own governments which implement local laws and regulations (jurisdictional right) and administrate over economic, social and cultural affairs in their region. These governments operate largely independently from the central government.

Autonomous regions (Xinjiang, Inner Mongolia, Tibet, Ningxia, Guangxi) have a higher percentage of ethnic minority groups, along with their own government. In theory these regions enjoy more legislative rights than regular provinces and have special regulations such as the non-imposition of the one-child policy. In practice the autonomy is quite limited.

Municipalities (Beijing, Chongqing, Shanghai, Tianjin) are higher level cities which enjoy provincial-level status. In Beijing, under the direct administration of the central government, municipalities were established to take the lead in the region's development.

Special Administrative Regions (SAR) (Hong Kong, Macau) operate under the principle of "one country, two economic systems". Their political system is different from mainland China and officially labeled as capitalistic with their Basic Law stipulating that both SARs shall have a "high degree of autonomy" until at least 2047 (Hong Kong) and 2049 (Macau). Both SARs maintain an individual legal system, police force, monetary system, customs policy, and immigration policy while the Chinese government is responsible for foreign relations and military defense.

© Springer International Publishing Switzerland 2015

H.R. Randau, O. Medinskaya, *China Business 2.0*, Management for Professionals,
DOI 10.1007/978-3-319-07677-5_37

37.2 Ethnic Groups and Language

The earliest widely accepted emergence of Chinese writing dates back to the inscriptions on oracle bones during the reign of King Wu Ding (1250–1192 B.C.). The official amount of characters in the Chinese language is debated by scholars, but is roughly 56,000. Only about 3,000 are in common use, and even learning 1,000 characters will allow one to understand 90 % of Chinese writing.

The official language of China—often referred to as the "*Han*-language"—is Mandarin, the language spoken in Beijing. It is the native language to more than 70 % of the Chinese population. However, autonomous regions and many other ethnic groups have their own native languages. Local dialects like Shanghainese and Cantonese (in South China and Hong Kong) are also widespread even though the increased economic and cultural flow across China has boosted the use of Mandarin in recent years.

China officially recognizes 56 ethnic groups in the PRC. Since the vast majority of China is of *Han* descent, ethnic minorities are synonymous with "non-*Han*" Chinese.

Officially, minority groups comprise about 8.5% of the population. Minorities are located primarily in the south, west, and north of China while most of eastern China is considered officially *Han*. The largest shares of these minority groups live in China's 5 Autonomous Regions.

38 Political System: The One-Party Nation

China's civil servants and government apparatus remain inefficient in many ways. Government jobs are coveted positions, since they are well-paid and offer excellent pension packages. Nevertheless, low performance and slow service are condoned. Time-consuming and excessive bureaucratic hurdles, long waits for permits and licenses, as well as confusing regulations are the norm, not a rarity.

All federal power within the PRC is divided between the Chinese Communist Party (CCP), the state government apparatus, and the People's Liberation Army (PLA). Many of China's leaders hold multiple positions at the same time. For instance, the president is often the general secretary of the CCP and head of the Central Military Commission. These interwoven but distinctly different divisions of power between the Party, government and the PLA make the political process complex and hierarchy unclear. Therefore, it can be difficult to determine who has authority to set or implement specific policies.

38.1 Chinese Communist Party

The PRC is effectively a single-party socialist republic governed by the CCP, which has ruled the Chinese mainland since 1949. Although other minor parties exist, they are essentially powerless because the CCP's leadership role is affirmed by the constitution. Other parties must be authorized by the CCP and thus may only contribute through consultation.

The CCP has over 85 million members and is open to any Chinese citizen over the age of 18 willing to accept and abide by the Party's constitution and policies. Its highest authority is the Political Bureau; the rest of the Party's formal structure consists of local, municipal, and provincial party congresses and committees. The most important body in this structure of congresses is the National Party Congress which convenes once every 5 years to set the country's overall policy direction and choose the members of the Party's Political Bureau (Fig. 38.1).

© Springer International Publishing Switzerland 2015

H.R. Randau, O. Medinskaya, *China Business 2.0*, Management for Professionals,
DOI 10.1007/978-3-319-07677-5_38

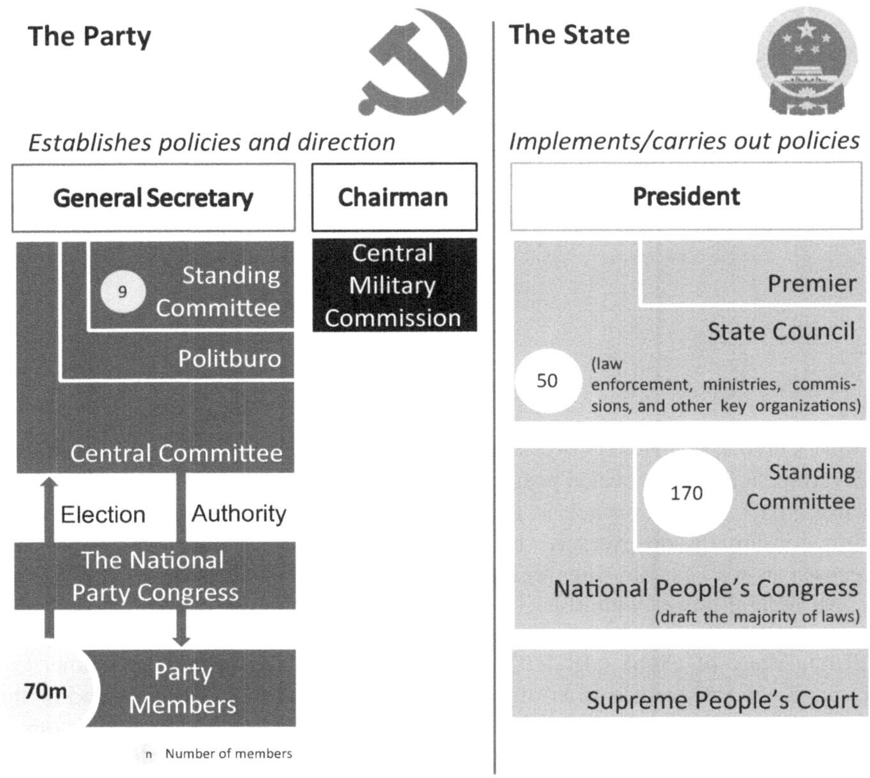

Fig. 38.1 Breakdown of the political system

38.2 State Government

The government is divided into two parts: a central bureaucracy and a geographic system of regional and local governments.

The State Council, as the executive arm of the government, functions as the cabinet of the PRC government. It is headed by the premier and composed of ministers, State Councilors, the governor of the People's Bank of China, and the auditor general of the National Audit Office. Due to the large size of the State Council (about 35 people), the daily government administration is mainly handled by the smaller State Councils Standing Committee, which usually consists of nine people.

China's governing bodies are divided according to activity. For example, the Ministry of Commerce oversees all business and commerce. Despite their effective subordination to the State Council and CCP, the ministries wield strong power in interpreting, implementing, and overseeing policies, and often operate independently. The ministries are organized into hierarchical layers with offices at the provincial and local levels, each with a significant degree of power and freedom (accounting for many of the government's enforcement problems). Each minister usually manages his or her ministry like a top executive because his or her political future is closely tied to its success.

38.3 National People's Congress

The National People's Congress (NPC), with 3,000 members, is constitutionally the highest legislative authority in China. In reality, however, the NPC is a largely symbolic organization. Its deputies are not popularly elected, but selected for 5-year terms by the next lower tier of people's congresses—deputies at the provincial and municipal level—and by members of the armed forces. The candidate pool for these elections is pre-approved by the Party, and the entire process is overseen by CCP election committees.

The NPC meets annually for 15 days in the spring to approve major new laws, establish the budget, set government policy, and select leadership. The first year of new legislation is the most important because this is when the PRC's president, premier, and cabinet-level officials are elected and when a 5-year plan is endorsed. The NPC president's power is mostly ceremonial and is limited to two 5 year terms. His effective responsibility is to promulgate the legislation adopted by the NPC.

38.4 People's Liberation Army

The People's Liberation Army (PLA) is led by two institutions. Nominally, the State Central Military Commission of the PRC, a state entity elected by the NPC, exercises control of the PLA. In reality, the Party-controlled Central Military Commission (CMC) commands military decisions; the memberships of the two commissions, however, are usually identical.

TIPS, OPPORTUNITIES, and WARNINGS

Tip: Build close relationships with local authorities

Although China's economy has become more permissive in several markets, it remains government-controlled. Almost nothing can be done without government involvement. A tight network of contacts with government officials is critical for your business success. Finding and building the right relationships with the government can especially helpful in understanding how rules and regulations are interpreted, understood, and implemented by local authorities.

Suggestions for Further Reading

Shambaugh, D. (Ed.). (2008). *China's communist party: Atrophy and adaptation.* Berkley: University of California Press.

Philosophy and Religion 39

Confucianism, Taoism, and Legalism have endured millennia of regime changes to shape Chinese life, morals, and social structures, and their core tenants continue to influence the Chinese people today.

39.1 Confucianism

Confucianism, an ethical and philosophical system, first came to being through its namesake, Confucius (552–479 B.C.), who lived in a time when China was divided into different empires and desperately needed a solid social order. Confucius proposed that a hierarchical ruling system be applied throughout society. The family, being the smallest unit of society, would serve as a model for larger social constructs.

According to his philosophy, each individual should be dutiful, honorable, rule abiding, and even-tempered. These virtues were manifested through filial obedience, loyalty to friends, and respects for elders and authority. The primacy of old over young and the superior over the subordinate was crucial, and later exploited by China's ruling elite.

Today, Confucian influence is fundamentally integrated into Chinese culture. In the household, Confucian sentiments create powerful, if not egotistical, senses of family loyalty. The father is the family leader and children— particularly the eldest son—view serving and obeying their parents and family elders as their most important obligation. This traditional family structure is strongest in rural areas today.

Confucian respect for hierarchy, social status, and personal relationships plays an important role in daily life and in business. Respecting personal and family connections can take priority over connections to companies, institutions or even laws. The strength of this social structure gives highly regarded people immense power, such that when an important leader leaves a company, his subordinates may follow suit.

© Springer International Publishing Switzerland 2015

H.R. Randau, O. Medinskaya, *China Business 2.0*, Management for Professionals,
DOI 10.1007/978-3-319-07677-5_39

Confucian influence also pervades the education system. Confucius taught that superiors should lead by example and emphasized that such exemplary behavior could only be institutionalized by repetitive education.

39.2 Taoism

Founded by Lao Zi in the sixth century B.C., Taoism is both a philosophy and a religion. Taoist thought generally focuses on nature, the relationship between humanity and the cosmos, health, longevity, and action through non-action. According to Taoism, all life in the universe shares a two-sided life-force called yin (dark side, associated with femininity, passiveness, water, earth and moon) and yang (light side, associated with masculinity, aggressiveness, fire, sky and the sun), which together must find an equal balance in the universe.

39.3 Legalism

Legalism is a pragmatic political philosophy. It assumes that all people are inherently bad, and necessitates strict laws and harsh punishments to maintain peace and order.

TIPS, OPPORTUNITIES, and WARNINGS

Tip: Learn to operate within the "Magic Triangle"

The key to operating within Chinese society is to understand and respect the "Magic Triangle" of harmony, status, and family. With these three in mind, most situations, customs, and cultural aspects can be understood or brought into context. Respecting, nurturing, and internalizing these characteristics when doing business in China will be essential for your success.

Suggestions for Further Reading

Bell, D. A. (2008). *China's new confucianism: Politics and everyday life in a changing society*. Princeton: Princeton Press.

40 The Importance of Family

Family plays a primary role in Chinese society, providing a network of safety, support and unity for its members. The Chinese are devoted to the well-being, stability, and continuity of their family, fostering a collectivist rather than individualist family environment.

40.1 Chinese Names

Family commitment is notably apparent in the protocol of name-giving, where the family name is always listed before the given name and holds special significance. There are about 3,500 Chinese family names used nowadays, but half of the Chinese population shares one of only 20 surnames with Wang, Zhang and Li being the most popular.[1]

Chinese first names have always had a special meaning. They often express the best wishes for the new-born child, such as Lì (Beautiful) and Jiàn (Healthy). It is also popular for Chinese names to refer to the child's birth place, like Jing (Beijing), nature, like Qiū (Autumn) and Yǔ (Rain), while others embody the hope of virtue, like Ǎi (friendly).

Lately, it has become very popular to adopt a western name in addition to the Chinese one. For those working with foreigners, this has proved very helpful, as the foreigners no longer have trouble pronouncing the Chinese names. It is also partly due to the tendency that foreign names are regarded as modern. Since the individuals chose the western name themselves and the Chinese are used to meaningful given first names, this sometimes leads to people choosing English names that seem weird to native English speakers, such as Panda or Rainbow. Some people even get their names from well-known American movies such as Rocky or Scarlett.

[1] According to the National Citizen Identity Information Center.

© Springer International Publishing Switzerland 2015

H.R. Randau, O. Medinskaya, *China Business 2.0*, Management for Professionals,
DOI 10.1007/978-3-319-07677-5_40

40.2 The Extended Family

Even in the business environment, key positions are often occupied by members of the family who owns the enterprise in order to ensure trust and reliability. This importance of family largely stems from traditional Confucian values, wherein the family was the focal point of society.

Not surprisingly, most Chinese still live in traditional extended families: it is common for households to contain two or even three generations of adults living under one roof. When young people move to urban settings, often families follow, even travelling great distances to reunite in one residence.

Despite the continued prevalence of extended households, new realities—common to industrialized countries worldwide—are emerging. As urban areas develop, households are separating and household sizes are falling. Increased time is spent in bachelorhood, particularly by the young, urban populations. Citizens are willing to postpone marriage and family building in favor of education and job experience, and the average age at which women have their first child is also increasing. As a result, young people and women have more time for recreation and increasingly participate in entertainment and travel. These new norms are changing the tone of the family, and are making peers rather than familiar relationships more and more influential.[2]

Weddings remain a significant part of Chinese family life, building strong bonds of *guanxi* and strengthening the family nucleus. Though arranged marriages are no longer legal (they were banned in the 1950's by Mao, who considered them a feudal tradition), parents and family members still hold substantial influence in the search for and selection of marriage partners. Matchmaking events are now becoming quite popular—the largest Shanghai matchmaking party in 2012 attracted 30,000 singles accompanied by concerned parents. Usually, family background (status, wealth, property ownership) is carefully weighed and matched before young people meet. Though the young bachelors and bachelorettes ultimately have the final say, these suggested matches can put considerable pressure on them, as they are forced to attend more and more blind dates arranged by their family.

Divorce today is a simple formality that either party can apply for. A more tolerant public attitude and an increasingly affluent society have catalyzed an increase in break-ups, with annual numbers jumping from 200,000 in the 1970's to 3.1 million in 2012.[3] Affairs, which have been a long-ingrained motif in Chinese history, are one of the most common reasons for these splits. Many Chinese men are more open about them than their western counterparts.[4]

---

[2] McKinsey Consumer & Shopper Insights: Meet the 2020 Chinese Consumer, March 2012, can be found at: www.mckinseychina.com

[3] China Statistical Yearbook (www.stats.gov.cn).

[4] Hershatter, Gail, Women in China's Long Twentieth Century (Berkeley: University of California Press, 2007).

From Collectivism to Individualism 41

Under the planned economic system, most goods and services were distributed to various places of employment, called *danwei*. Apartment housing, welfare benefits, and even necessary items like sandals were all rationed in this manner. In general, the consumption of goods was highly regulated through government quotas and ration coupons and special goods such as bikes could only be bought with vouchers. Even if one had the money, no voucher meant no bike. These policies reduced socio-economic inequalities (except disparities between urban and rural regions) but also limited individualism. At the time, most of the population wore similar clothes, sported similar hairstyles, and rode the same bicycles.

Today, individualism has emerged as an important ideal and consumption has become the means of expressing social identity. Since wealth perception is highly valued, citizens spend comparably large sums on highly visible status symbols such as smart phones, tablet computers, bags, clothing, and cars. Younger generations in particular, partly driven by the wish to be taken seriously, display their wealth openly: housewives drive expensive sports cars in congested cities, children flaunt clothes from exclusive brands (choosing prestigious and expensive over functionally identical clothing), and expensive ice cream is purchased publicly as a demonstration of affluence. It is no surprise that China has become a major luxury goods market.[1]

Many reasons have been offered for this preoccupation with consumerism:

- A compensation for the lack of political freedom. It is certainly also a reaction to the conformism and homogeneous "massified consumption" (Lu 2000) that characterized life in the pre-reform era
- A signaling of social status connected to the concept of face (*mianzi*)
- An assertion of modernity

[1] Consumer goods: The Mystery of the Chinese Consumer, 07.07.2011, can be found at:www.economist.com

© Springer International Publishing Switzerland 2015
H.R. Randau, O. Medinskaya, *China Business 2.0*, Management for Professionals,
DOI 10.1007/978-3-319-07677-5_41

- Active promotion from the government: redefining oneself through shopping is approved from the top as it generates economic growth and stabilizes society (Elfick 2011).

Despite the apparent materialism and obsession with status symbols, Chinese consumers remain grounded by financial constraints. In public, it may seem that the Chinese are rather extravagant spenders because they are always concerned with their public status. However, most Chinese consumers are much more price-sensitive when they are not in the public eye.

INSIGHT: Arnaud Debane, Superbrands

30 years of brand building in China

Chinese people above 60 years old can hardly recall 10 brands from their childhood; back then, there were few manufactured products and most of them were unbranded. Two generations later, finding a Chinese lady who can't quote 10 luxury brands would be a challenge.

As most consumer product categories and brands did not exist 20 or 30 years ago, we don't see much brand legacy across generations in China. In mature western markets, brands tend to pass from generation to generation: if your parents used Colgate, you are much more likely to buy Colgate for the rest of your life. The opposite often takes place in China where we actually see numerous cases of common FMCG products and brands introduced by children in the household.

Little brand history

With little history and legacy in consumer minds, local and foreign brands entering the market are presented with the opportunity to introduce their brand credentials from a blank piece of paper. When setting up in China, foreign brands should not be shy to revisit their positioning, messages and offering, especially if there is no demand overlap with their home market base.

Until few years ago, brands were focused on creating new needs, growing their market base while at the same time keeping leadership in their category. There was a clear advantage to early comers with a long term vision and means to back it up such as Nescafé who introduced instant coffee to China in the mid 80s and has been defining since then coffee consumption and lifestyle. Developing market awareness was – and still is in many consumer markets – the main focus of brands, through massive (and often simplistic) ad campaign, often riding on the fame of local celebrities acting as 'brand ambassadors'.

Middle class and wealthy consumers

Along with the emergence of middle class and wealthy consumers, Chinese people started to turn to brands as symbols of lifestyle, social status or personality. In a Chinese culture that traditionally values uniformity, brands provide a unique and accessible way for individuals to state their personality. Today, as consumer markets are more and more sophisticated and competitive, we see some brands succeeded in building viable niches and differentiate along a set of values.

In the setting, brand awareness is less relevant – customer interaction and engagement are the names of the game. Social media turns out to be the ideal platform to support such interaction; it enables a brand to engage directly and efficiently target customers and provide a platform for customers to express themselves. Consumer brands are now investing heavily on ever more creative and sophisticated campaigns combining hard advertisements, couponing, promotions and social media to build up some emotional connection.

At the same time, large pockets of the country are still shopping for necessities and are not sensitive to such campaigns (rural China still makes about ½ of the country's population). On top of fierce competition, sudden shifts in market conditions, the diversity of Chinese consumer represents another challenge for consistent brand building across the country.

References

Elfick, J. (2011). Class formation and consumption among middle-class professionals in Shenzhen. *Journal of Current Chinese Affairs, 40*(1), 187–211.

Lu, H. (2000). To be relatively comfortable in an Egalitaria society. In D. Davis (Ed.), *The consumer revolution in Urban China*. Berkeley: University of California Press.

Generations of Change 42

Population demographics play a major role in any analysis of Chinese society because different age groups have different values and display very different behavioral patterns.

Younger generations are more open to foreign cultures, new technologies, and an ever changing dynamic global environment. The young Chinese show outward signs of Westernization, but below the surface they remain deeply rooted in their traditional Chinese values and perceptions (Chap. 39): they still prioritize responsibility for the family, building of relationships (*guanxi*), striving for achievement, academic and workplace resilience, and maintaining interpersonal harmony, with hierarchy as the basis for social structure and interaction. It seems as Chinese modernize, they do not westernize (Lynton and Thøgersen 2006).

42.1 1950s and Older

This generation has experienced the harsh conditions of the Cultural Revolution in the late 1960s and early 1970s. Not surprisingly given their historic experience, economic safety is their major concern. Traditional Chinese values are important to them and they are strongly focused on their families. People of this generation tend to be cautious spenders: if they have any savings, they devote the money to their family, especially their grand-children, as opposed to consuming the money themselves.

42.2 1960s and 1970s

Relative to previous generations, those born in the 1960s and 1970s already tend to be much more open. Having never lived through a recession, this generation is influenced by a lifetime of economic growth. Accordingly, their attitude towards the future tends to be optimistic and they enjoy their success by investing in

© Springer International Publishing Switzerland 2015

H.R. Randau, O. Medinskaya, *China Business 2.0*, Management for Professionals,
DOI 10.1007/978-3-319-07677-5_42

housing, cars, and even travel. However, compared to other countries, this generation of Chinese remains generally conservative spenders. Since they grew up in a time of shortages they are primarily focused on building economic security (Barton et al. 2013).

Deeply rooted *Confucian* influence has persisted in this age group: they actively support their parents and concentrate most of their efforts on their children's education. Focus on the well-being of their nuclear family clearly has a higher priority than self-expression and consumption.

42.3 1980s and Younger

Unlike any of the above generations, these young Chinese were born under the one-child policy. Those raised as single children in traditional extended families (Chap. 40) in urban areas display particularly different behavioral patterns. Having received the full attention of six adults throughout their lives, many of them seem spoiled—an effect referred to as the "little emperor syndrome".

Born in a period when China's economic reforms were gathering steam, household income and property values have steadily risen throughout their adult lives and they are extremely optimistic about their future prospects: approximately two thirds believe their incomes will continue to grow significantly over the next 5 years (Frijters et al. 2012).

This group is also generally well educated[1] and used to performance pressure. Their lifestyles share many similarities with those of their western counterparts, such the extensive use of technologies and the wearing of branded clothing. Though often perceived as selfish or self-centered, this generation still feels a strong responsibility to their family and holds on to core Chinese values.

The major difference is that this generation resists discipline more than previous generations and is less willing to accept ingrained hierarchies. The highly educated are especially prone to challenge the status of hierarchy and request performance related reasons for accepting authority. New emphasis on critical thinking in Chinese education is causing difficulties in the workplace, as it contradicts the traditional core value of maintaining harmony (Fig. 42.1).

[1] According to studies such as those by Posten and Falbo of the Guttmacher Institute, China's solo children perform significantly better academically than peers with siblings. See more Falbo, Toni, and Poston, Dudley L., *The Academic, Personality, and Physical Outcomes of Only Children in China*, Child Development, 1993, Pg. 18-35

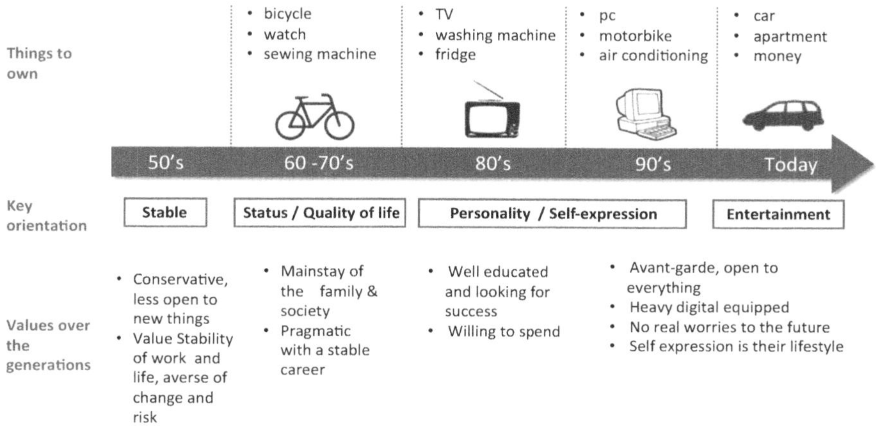

Fig. 42.1 Generations of change

References

Barton, D., Chen, Y., & Jin, A. (2013). China's next chapter: Mapping China's middle class. *McKinsey Quarterly, 3*, 54–60.

Frijters, P., Liu, A., & Meng, X. (2012). Are optimistic expectations keeping the Chinese happy? *Journal of Economic Behavior & Organization, 81*(1), 159–171.

Lynton, N., & Thøgersen, K. H. (2006). How china transforms an executive's mind. *Organizational Dynamics, 35*(2), 170–181.

43 Etiquette: Dos and Don'ts

43.1 Meeting and Greeting

Meeting and greeting in Chinese business culture is rather formal and follows a protocol that western managers would be advised to adhere to. Because Chinese value seniority, participants are expected to enter a meeting room in hierarchical order. The meeting begins with introductions (during which it is polite to remain standing), with company or group leaders being introduced first. The greeting procedure usually starts with the shaking of hands (not too vigorously) and a slight nod of the head or a bow. Throughout the meeting, formal titles should be used as a sign of respect. Chinese associates are referred to as Mr. or Miss, or any other title such as Dr. together with the surname, even outside the business realm.

Then, business cards are exchanged. The card should be held with both hands and presented in such a way that the name is facing the recipient. Ideally, cards should be translated in Chinese and include the name, title, company and e-mail address. Bilingual cards should be presented with the visible side in the native language of the recipient.

After reception it is customary to read over the card in order to memorize people's name and title. The card needs to be treated with great respect and it is a faux pas to write on it or put it directly away in a wallet or pocket. On Chinese business cards, the family name always appears first.

Senior persons should start the conversation and lead the meeting discussion; interruptions from subordinates may be considered highly inappropriate. A pleasant atmosphere should be created before a meeting starts: a few words in Chinese, positive impressions about the progress of projects, small talk about changing and improving life in China, or some inoffensive jokes usually do the trick.

© Springer International Publishing Switzerland 2015

H.R. Randau, O. Medinskaya, *China Business 2.0*, Management for Professionals,
DOI 10.1007/978-3-319-07677-5_43

TIPS, OPPORTUNITIES, and WARNINGS

Tip: Respect seniority

Pay special attention to the concept of seniority during any meetings or business situations. Based on Confucian values, priority is expected to be given to high-ranking individuals in seating arrangements, meeting discussions, and even day-to- day office life.

43.2 Body Language

- The Chinese are not keen on physical contact, but same-sex Chinese often touch each other as an expression of friendship. Also, physical contact is common when a host is guiding a guest
- The Chinese do not use their hands when speaking. An open palm should be used to point but not the index finger. Expansive gestures and unusual facial expressions should be avoided
- The Chinese smile very often, even when they are in a difficult situation. Many feel showing a sad face in a sad situation is no help
- It is considered impolite and aggressive to look people straight in the eye; instead people look only briefly in the eye

43.3 Gift Giving

In China, gift giving is a good way to build *guanxi*, and does not carry negative connotations when doing business. Giving gifts is also connected to the concept of *face* (Chap. 46), and any action which may cause embarrassment, discomfort, and the loss of *face* for both the recipient and the giver must be avoided. As with favors, business gifts are always reciprocated. Here are some important gift giving tips:

- Gifts must not necessarily be expensive but should be of good quality; cheap gifts damage the reputation of the giver
- Gifts should always be exchanged during celebrations
- When giving a gift at negotiations, be sure to present the gift before the talks are closed
- Birthday gifts should be given before rather than after the actual birthday. Late gifts are seen as disrespectful while early gifts are just the opposite
- A gift must be wrapped and always presented in person: never send a gift to a Chinese person by mail
- If visiting an organization, it is appropriate to present one gift to the whole group. If several gifts are to be presented, it is important to consider the

	Appropriate	Inappropriate
Gifts	• Pens (avoid red ink) • Paperweights • Calculators • Chocolate • Wine and Spirits	• Money • "Made in Asia" items if you are Western • Clocks, kerchiefs, straw sandals (symbolizes death) • Knives, blades or scissors (symbolizes severing of relationships)
Colors	• Pink and yellow for happiness • Red for good fortune	• blue • black • white
Numbers	• 8 stands for luck • 3 stands for vitality and upturn • Both numbers and quantities have these connotations (the number 8 and / or 8 chocolates imply luck for the recipient)	• 4 and 14 ("4" and "death" have similar pronunciations and associations in Mandarin) • Similarly, both numbers and quantities can also have negative connotations.

Fig. 43.1 Guide to gift giving

hierarchy within the group and to ensure that the more important person receives the more valuable gift!

- According to Chinese etiquette, the gift is offered and received with two hands

If the receiver does not want to appear greedy he/she might refuse the gift initially. The giver should continue to offer the gift and tell the receiver that he/she will not be happy until it has been accepted. Usually the receiver will thank the giver and set the gift aside to open it later. It is considered impolite to open gifts immediately in front of others: this avoids the loss of face for the recipient and the giver in the case of an inappropriate gift (Fig. 43.1).

TIPS, OPPORTUNITIES, and WARNINGS

Tip: Support your business partner's gift-giving efforts

Don't be surprised when Chinese people want to buy you a gift, they may ask what gift you prefer. This approach is used in order to save *face* and avoid negative/unpleasant surprises. If you do not have a specific wish, it is wise to ask for items that show your appreciation of the Chinese culture, such as ink paintings or tea.

Suggestions for Further Reading

Brahm, L. J. (2007). *The art of the deal in China: A practical guide to business etiquette and the 36 martial strategies employed by Chinese businessmen and officials in China*. Tokyo: Tuttle Publishing.

44 Chinese Festivals: Knowing the Roots

44.1 Moon Calendar

Traditionally, China has always used the lunisolar calendar with month length determined by lunar phases. But with the end of the Empire in 1911, China switched to the more international Gregorian, or sun calendar—as used in all western countries—for standard dating. The lunisolar calendar, however, continues to hold influence. One of its most important influences is on the dating of festivals and holidays. These festivals, including the Chinese New Year and Moon Festival, fall on different dates of the Gregorian calendar each year because the two calendars have different year lengths. In contrast to traditional festivals, state holidays follow the Gregorian calendar (→see Fig. 44.1).

The lunisolar calendar still significantly affects the way tradition-conscious Chinese schedule their lives. Many of them still use the traditional calendar to schedule personal events such as marriage, the day they take out loans, and even haircuts, believing that if they do something at the right time on the right moon it will bring them luck and blessing in their endeavors.

44.2 Chinese New Year (Chinese Spring Festival)

The Chinese New Year, or Spring Festival, is the most important traditional Chinese festival. It begins on the 1st day of the 1st lunar month, and marks the year of a new animal on the Chinese zodiac.

The Chinese Zodiac is based on a 12-year cycle, with each year marked by a different animal imparting its distinct characteristic. There are also animal signs assigned by month, by day, and by hour. Many Chinese believe that the year of birth is the primary factor in determining personality traits, physical and mental attributes, and degree of success and happiness in life.

© Springer International Publishing Switzerland 2015
H.R. Randau, O. Medinskaya, *China Business 2.0*, Management for Professionals,
DOI 10.1007/978-3-319-07677-5_44

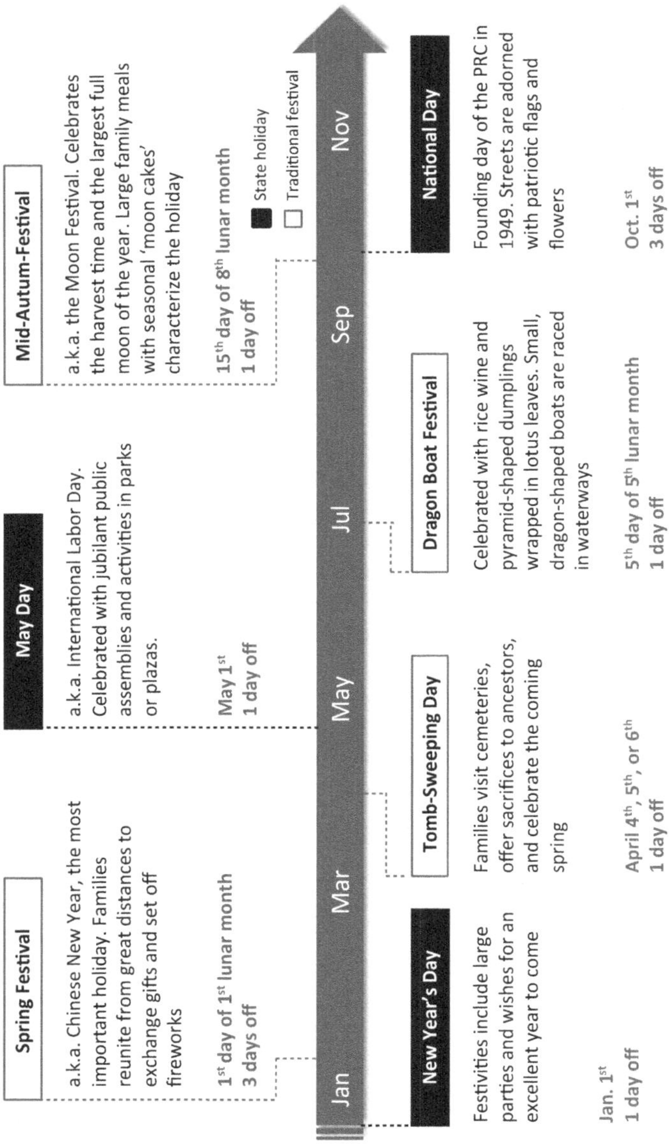

Fig. 44.1 Timeline of major holidays and festivals

The Spring Festival Week is the largest of China's two annual Golden Weeks (the other being National Day Week), where Chinese employees get at least 3 days off work. Most people take additional days off, joining 2 weekends with the holidays to create week long vacations. During this time, the world's largest annual migration occurs as millions of Chinese families do their utmost to meet up and spend the holiday together, regardless of how far apart they live.

The New Year is a time centered on family reunions. Family members get together to visit and share meals. Like important holidays in western countries, the Chinese New Year's Celebration is firmly rooted in tradition. It is believed that following these traditions and customs will bring success to the individual and good luck to Chinese society in the New Year.

One New Year's tradition involves widespread use of the color red, including the wearing of red clothes, decorating the home with poems written on red paper, and exchanging monetary gifts contained in red envelopes. The color red can be found everywhere at that time of the year because it symbolizes fire which was in ancient times believed to ward off evil spirits. Even the fireworks welcoming the New Year go back to a custom where the cracking flames from lit bamboo stalks would frighten off evil spirits.

44.3 Moon Festival

The historic moon or mid-autumn festival celebrates the glories and mysteries of the moon, and is largely a traditional ode to the moon's role in establishing water reservoirs and increasing soil fertility, thus determining the success of the overall harvest. One of the most recognizable traditions of this festival is the trading of moon cakes—small circular pastries usually eaten in wedges along with Chinese tea. These moon cakes are exchanged prior to and during moon festival—as a gift to business clients, to celebrate with colleagues in the workplace, and to kick off festivities amongst friends and family.

TIPS, OPPORTUNITIES, and WARNINGS

Tip: Understand the importance of Red Envelops

Gifts presented at social and family gatherings, such as weddings, or on holidays, such as Chinese New Year, are presented in red envelopes. Inside the red envelop you will always find cash.

Please remember that the amount should end in an even digit (amounts ending in odd digits are used for funerals). Do not use the number four, as the pronunciation of the word "four" sounds like the Chinese word "death".

45 Business Banquets

Banquets are an excellent basis for forming *guanxi*. Often, negotiation breakthroughs are made during these social occasions. Rules for proper banquet behavior vary from region to region, so the following paragraphs only outline the basic rules that must be followed in order to avoid embarrassing faux pas.

45.1 Timing

Banquets have definite beginnings and endings, typically lasting for two hours. Evening banquets start around 6:00 p.m. in a private room in a restaurant. Chinese usually arrive early at banquets and greet all the guests starting with the host. Arriving late for a formal banquet is considered extremely rude. The host usually arrives at least 30 min early to finalize arrangements for his/her guests.

45.2 Seating

Since rank and hierarchy play an important role in China, the leader of a group should enter the event first, followed by other group members in rank order. Guests should wait until they are shown where to sit, since they will also be seated according to rank. Generally, the host sits facing the door, with the honored guest seated to his/her right. Everyone else is seated in descending order of rank, which means that the guest with lowest status is sitting with his/her back to the door (Fig. 45.1).

© Springer International Publishing Switzerland 2015

H.R. Randau, O. Medinskaya, *China Business 2.0*, Management for Professionals,
DOI 10.1007/978-3-319-07677-5_45

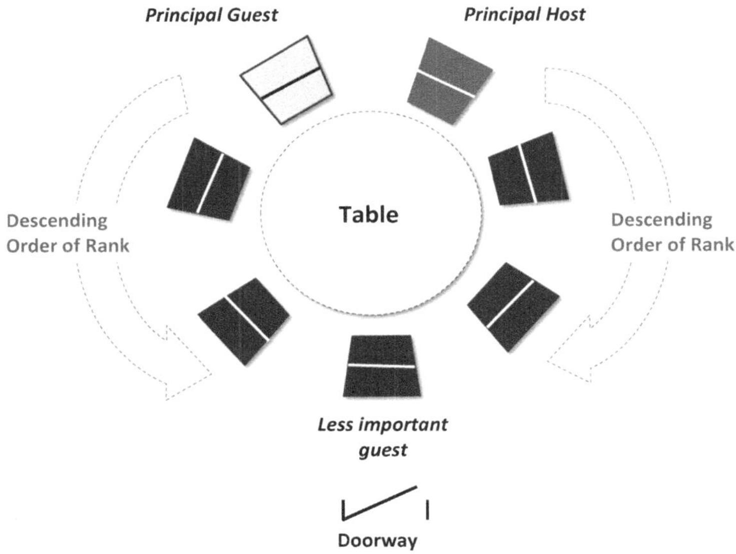

Fig. 45.1 Business banquet seating

45.3 Structure

The formal progress of a Chinese banquet is led by the principal host and it is customary for the principal guest to reciprocate his/her behavior. The principle host begins the banquet with a welcoming toast, after which the principal guest says some words thanking and respecting the host. Then the formal meal begins.

The principal host is the first person at the table to begin eating. Often he/she takes the first piece of the most valued food and puts it on the guest of honor's plate as a token of friendship. Toasts and short speeches are given throughout the meal while participants share different dishes from a central, circular turntable. The greater the number of courses, the harder the Chinese host is trying to impress the guest. Decoration is important but the quality of food is even more important. The guest should taste all the dishes offered and should not be surprised if some food is left over: Chinese associate serving too much food with being a good host; if all dishes are completely gone, it gives the impression that the guests are still hungry.

The meal typically closes with a serving of rice or noodles followed by a serving of fruit and/or tea.

The guests of honor should then make a motion to leave, giving the principle host the chance to close the event at the scheduled time; it is considered rude to keep others at the banquet past the designated ending time. Finally, guests should thank their host and depart after the host says some final words.

45.4 Toasting

Toasting is a fundamental part of the Chinese banquet and is begun by the principal host. Toasts are then proposed throughout the meal. The toaster usually stands to speak, while the others are expected to stop eating and drinking to accept and toast in response. The glass should be held high by the right hand and supported by the left hand at the bottom. When clinking glasses, one should hold the glass lower than that of the host to show respect. Many people can toast to one person, but only the host should toast to many people.

Toasts are typically short (usually 10–20 s), with common subjects being thanks to the host, friendship, future success, cooperation, mutual benefits, comments on the visit, good luck and health. A popular toast is *ganbei* (empty glass), where the drink is downed at once.

Glasses are kept full during the meal to allow toasting. It is customary to refill glasses to full level even if they were not completely empty. Usually the member of the hosting group closest to the teapot or bottle pours drinks for the guests. The guest should reciprocate the refill in the course of the banquet as a gesture of thanks to the host.

45.5 Alcohol

The Chinese have a strong drinking culture. Sharing of alcohol is an important facet in developing trust. This is the reason why large quantities of beer, wine, or Chinese white liquors are often served. *Baijiu*, a potent rice or sorghum distilled liquor (40–60 % alcohol by volume), is the most common. *Baijiu* should not be sipped, but rather downed at once.

45.6 Conversation

Conversation at the banquet is generally light, with common topics being the weather, economic progress in China, sightseeing, cultural highlights, and heritage. Controversial subjects such as politics, religion, sex, Tibet, and Taiwan should be avoided. Questions relating to age, education and even salary level are not uncommon; however, divorces and non-marital children should not be part of the conversation as they indicate unreliability. To avoid disturbing the harmony of the event, it may sometimes be necessary to answer a question with a white lie.

45.7 Payment

Splitting the bill is considered crude while being the one that pays is considered an honor. According to custom, the person that extends an invitation or the highest ranking person is the person who pays. It is considered tasteless to pay in front of the guests, so usually the host excuses himself and pays the bill privately. Tipping is not practiced in China.

45.8 Table Manners in China

- On a typical dining table there is a cup, a bowl on a small dish, and chopsticks.
- Chinese do not eat directly from the serving dish. Chopsticks and serving spoons are both used to move food from serving bowls to one's individual bowl or plate before eating.
- The bowl is lifted and held with the left hand in order to eat comfortably in an upright position.
- Chopsticks should be placed on the holders that are provided or set across the (rice) bowl to indicate that one is finished.
- It is taboo to stick chopsticks straight up in the bowl or the center of the rice because this resembles incense-sticks for the dead—an omen of bad luck.
- Gesturing with a chopstick is considered rude.
- It is a faux pas to eat food that has fallen off the plate onto the table or tablecloth.
- Dishes with fish and chicken are often full of bones. The Chinese often spit out bones on the dish or even on the tablecloth.
- Fish will be placed on the table with the head pointed at the honorable guest, and should not be turned over (another indication of bad luck).
- It is acceptable to belch and slurp during the meal—this is taken as a sign of appreciation.
- Talking while eating and picking teeth with a toothpick is customary.

TIPS, OPPORTUNITIES, and WARNINGS

Tip: Avoid controversial "delicacies"

Shark fin soup is a common feature at banquets. These sharks fins are served because many Chinese believe they heighten sexual ability (which has never been proven). Sharks continue to be killed at a rate of around 200 million per year, solely for their fins. As a result, several species of these sharks are now endangered.

Due to the cruel way in which shark fins are harvested (fins are cut off while the animals are alive and the sharks are thrown back into the water where they die eventually) and the subsequent marine ecological destruction, several luxury hotels have already banned shark fin soup in their restaurants.

It is your decision to accept such "delicacies". Informing the host in advance to eliminate shark fins or similar dishes (e.g. coral fish) helps to avoid conflict.

Tip: Excessive drinking can be avoided

If you do not wish to consume alcohol, inform the host before dinner starts. It is acceptable to avoid drinking entirely, but drinking a first glass and refusing to drink further can be considered rude and can amount to a loss of face for the host, because it gives the impression that you are not enjoying yourself. A good excuse to avoid excessive drinking would be to pretend you are a non-drinker or allergic to alcohol.

46 Social Concepts: Mianzi and Guanxi

46.1 Face (Mianzi)

"*Face*" or "*Mianzi*", is a social concept combining pride, reputation, and honor which greatly impacts personal success and social standing in China.

The Chinese are sensitive to gaining, maintaining and losing *face* in all aspects of life. The collective nature of Chinese society implies that the loss of *face* of one person affects not only the individual but also his or her environment. Thus, causing someone to lose face, even if unintentional, could seriously damage a relationship.

Face can be given to others through compliments, respect, and professionalism. Giving face earns respect and loyalty, but over-use can suggest insincerity. The following points will help to save face:

- Respect seniority (age and rank)
- Show no open anger
- Avoid confrontations and degrading language
- Never joke about someone who is not a close friend
- Do not criticize someone in public or single anyone out in a group situation. If criticism is necessary, pull the person aside and speak privately
- When reciprocating an invitation, it should at least equal the prior engagement in value

TIPS, OPPORTUNITIES, and WARNINGS

Tip: Learn to say "no" the Chinese way

To save *face*, sometimes it is better to give an indirect response, especially when conveying a negative answer. Phrases like, "that's an interesting idea," or "we will consider your thoughts," will usually be better received than a flat "no".

© Springer International Publishing Switzerland 2015

H.R. Randau, O. Medinskaya, *China Business 2.0*, Management for Professionals,
DOI 10.1007/978-3-319-07677-5_46

46.2 Connection (Guanxi)

Personal relationships are more important to business in China than they are in the West. The Chinese prefer to deal with people they trust or who come with good references from their friends. They believe that prospective business partners should build a personal relationship before starting with business dealings. This concept is called *guanxi*, which literally means "right relations and developing good feelings for each other".

Having a good *guanxi* network implies that one is well-connected, cooperative, and may ask for—and reciprocate—favors from these connections. Chinese view a favor as an investment that sooner or later will be repaid. Thus, it must carefully be gauged what one can possibly do in return before accepting a favor. One person's *guanxi* network gives him/her a form of social security as he/she can always expect help and support from friends.

To secure long-term business in China, it is therefore essential to acquire the right *guanxi* network. It may also be strategic to establish good *guanxi* with government officials who can speed up government approvals or provide legislative advice. Of course, it cannot be expected that officials will break laws because of good *guanxi*!

The following rules support the creation of *guanxi*:

- Follow through on promises and reciprocate (even breaking small promises such as not returning a call are considered extremely rude)
- Never offer monetary bribes, even when asking for a favor
- Learn about Chinese history, culture and language. This shows that one values the importance of personal relationships
- If a favor cannot be accommodated, refuse politely and respectfully so as not to cause offense. Even better, try and think of a fair compromise

TIPS, OPPORTUNITIES, and WARNINGS

Tip: Develop and maintain a good network

Guanxi plays a major role in business. Respectable leaders are expected to have strong and wide-reaching connections. Therefore, a good network is crucial for success. For example, in cases of legal uncertainty, those who have better *guanxi* often win their case.

Developing and nurturing *guanxi* bonds is an ongoing process that demands time and resources. Frequent contacts, small gifts, and dinner invitations are often required. Generally, it is wise to build relationships with persons of high rank first, since they can then influence their subordinates to cooperate.

Index

© Springer International Publishing Switzerland 2015

H.R. Randau, O. Medinskaya, *China Business 2.0*, Management for Professionals,
DOI 10.1007/978-3-319-07677-5

The manufacturer's authorised representative in the EU is Springer Nature Customer Service Centre GmbH, Europaplatz 3, 69115 Heidelberg, Germany. If you have any concerns regarding our products, please contact ProductSafety@springernature.com

Printed and bound by CPI Group (UK) Ltd, Croydon, CR0 4YY
30/09/2026
02225572-0008